GIT AND GITHUB ESSENTIALS

Version Control for Developers

THOMPSON CARTER

TABLE OF CONTENTS

INTRODUCTION

Mastering Git and GitHub: A Complete Guide for Developers

In today's world of software development, version control is not just a tool—it's the backbone of collaboration, workflow management, and maintaining code quality. Whether you are a solo developer working on an independent project or part of a large team collaborating on a complex system, version control systems like Git are indispensable. Git's flexibility, speed, and reliability have made it the de facto standard for version control, and its integration with GitHub, the world's leading platform for code collaboration, has revolutionized how developers work together.

However, while Git and GitHub are widely used, they remain underutilized or misunderstood by many developers. What seems like a simple command-line tool for tracking changes quickly evolves into a powerful system for managing collaborative workflows, automating processes, and scaling projects. This book, *Mastering Git and GitHub: A Complete Guide for Developers*, is your comprehensive guide to understanding not only the basics but also the advanced features of these tools. It is designed to take you from being a Git novice to a confident user who can leverage Git and GitHub to their full potential.

Why This Book Is Different

In the vast world of resources available on Git and GitHub, you'll find documentation, tutorials, and guides that explain how to use individual commands or features in isolation. However, very few resources provide a cohesive, step-by-step understanding of how to use Git and GitHub together as part of a complete, efficient development workflow. This book fills that gap by providing a structured, hands-on guide that explores Git's core functionality and GitHub's collaborative features, while also addressing best practices, advanced techniques, and real-world scenarios.

Whether you're just starting to use version control or you're a seasoned developer looking to refine your skills, this book offers something for everyone. Each chapter is written with practical examples that help solidify the concepts you'll need to become a proficient user of Git and GitHub. More importantly, it emphasizes how these tools fit into the bigger picture of software development, guiding you in creating a Git workflow tailored to your needs— whether you're managing your own solo projects or working within a team of developers.

Who Should Read This Book?

This book is intended for developers of all levels who want to master version control with Git and GitHub. If you're a beginner, don't worry—this book starts with the basics and builds on them progressively. If you're an experienced developer, you'll appreciate the advanced topics that delve into the complexities of Git's branching model, merge strategies, and integration with continuous integration/continuous deployment (CI/CD) systems.

You should read this book if:

- You are new to version control and want to understand how Git works.
- You want to level up your GitHub skills, especially for team collaboration and open-source contributions.
- You are managing a personal project and want to maintain a clean, organized version history.
- You are working on a team and want to implement Git workflows that streamline collaboration and reduce friction.
- You are interested in mastering advanced Git features like rebasing, cherry-picking, and submodules.

What You'll Learn

By the end of this book, you'll be able to confidently use Git and GitHub to:

- **Understand the fundamental concepts of version control**: You'll learn how Git tracks changes, how to create and manage branches, and how to merge and resolve conflicts efficiently.
- **Navigate and manage repositories on GitHub**: From creating repositories and making your first commit to

collaborating with others via pull requests, this book covers everything you need to know about GitHub's integration with Git.

- **Implement effective workflows for teams**: Learn best practices for managing code in a team environment, including the use of feature branches, pull requests, and continuous integration pipelines.

- **Utilize advanced Git features**: Dive into rebase, bisect, and advanced merge techniques, and discover how to optimize your workflow using Git hooks, Git tags, and submodules.

- **Leverage GitHub's powerful tools for collaboration**: You'll gain insight into GitHub's collaborative features like issues, project management, actions, and more to keep your projects organized and maintain high-quality code.

- **Troubleshoot and debug Git effectively**: Learn how to use Git's powerful debugging tools to track down issues, recover lost commits, and resolve common problems that arise in real-world workflows.

How This Book Is Organized

This book is divided into **three main parts** to provide a logical progression, starting with foundational concepts and building up to more advanced topics:

1. **Part 1: Getting Started with Git**
   This section introduces Git, covering essential concepts like commits, branches, and version history. You'll learn how to install and configure Git, make your first commits, and understand Git's basic commands. By the end of this section, you'll be comfortable using Git for personal version control.

2. **Part 2: Mastering GitHub for Collaboration**
   GitHub is the most popular platform for Git repositories, and this section focuses on how to make the most out of GitHub's collaboration features. You'll learn how to push and pull changes, use issues for tracking, work with pull requests, and implement workflows that help teams work together effectively. You'll also explore GitHub Actions for CI/CD and other advanced integrations.

3. **Part 3: Advanced Git Techniques**
   Once you've mastered the basics, this section dives deeper into advanced Git concepts. Topics like rebasing, merge strategies, managing large repositories, Git hooks, and using submodules will help you work more efficiently in complex environments. This section is geared toward developers who want to fine-tune their Git skills and integrate Git with larger project management and automation systems.

Real-World Examples

Throughout the book, you'll encounter real-world examples that illustrate how Git and GitHub are used in actual development environments. These examples show how to work with others in a collaborative setting, manage a project over time, and integrate Git with other tools like CI/CD platforms, project management software, and testing frameworks.

Why Git and GitHub Matter

The rise of open-source software, remote teams, and agile development practices has made Git and GitHub indispensable. Version control is no longer just for tracking code—it's about managing a project's lifecycle, facilitating collaboration, and keeping teams aligned. Whether you're managing a small hobby project or working in a large organization, understanding Git and GitHub is essential for keeping your work organized, efficient, and high quality.

Git is designed to handle everything from small-scale solo projects to massive, enterprise-level applications. GitHub makes collaboration seamless, with tools that help you work with contributors from all over the world. Together, these tools enable a level of productivity and organization that was once impossible.

By the end of this book, you will be well-equipped to tackle any Git or GitHub-related challenge, whether you're working on a solo project or part of a complex team effort. You'll be ready to collaborate, automate your workflows, and take full advantage of

Git's and GitHub's extensive capabilities. This book is designed to empower you as a developer, providing you with the knowledge and skills necessary to master version control, streamline your development process, and build better software.

CHAPTER 1: INTRODUCTION TO VERSION CONTROL

Version control is a fundamental practice in software development that allows developers to manage changes to code and track its history over time. It's a system that not only ensures data integrity but also supports collaboration, enables easy rollback to previous versions, and fosters transparency. In this chapter, we'll dive deep into the concept of version control, its importance, and how Git, in particular, plays a crucial role in modern software development.

The Need for Version Control

Before version control systems (VCS) became common in development workflows, managing changes to software code was a chaotic and error-prone process. Developers would work on the same files and, without proper tracking, could easily overwrite each other's work, leading to potential loss of data, inconsistent code, and endless hours of debugging to reconcile different versions.

Key Challenges without Version Control:

- **No historical record:** It becomes hard to trace back to earlier versions of code or understand why a change was made.

- **Loss of work:** Without a centralized system, developers can overwrite each other's work without realizing it.

- **Hard to collaborate:** In a team environment, coordinating efforts becomes increasingly difficult when multiple developers work on the same codebase simultaneously.

- **Inconsistent environments:** If each developer is working on a different version of the code, integrating all changes into a single, unified version becomes a nightmare.

Version control solves all of these problems by keeping track of changes in the code, allowing developers to work on different parts of a project simultaneously while ensuring that the final product remains stable and consistent.

Key Benefits of Version Control:

- **Tracking Changes:** Every change made to the code is stored along with a description of the change and who made it.

- **Collaboration:** Multiple developers can work on the same project without overwriting each other's work. Conflicts can be easily identified and resolved.

- **Reverting Changes:** Developers can easily roll back to previous versions of the codebase if a problem arises, ensuring a stable state of the project at all times.
- **Branching:** Developers can experiment with new features without affecting the main project, allowing them to create separate "branches" for testing and merging back once the work is finished.

Version control is not just for large-scale projects. Even small projects can benefit from version control to ensure better code organization, history tracking, and collaboration.

What is Git and Why It's Important

Git is a distributed version control system (DVCS), created by Linus Torvalds (the creator of Linux) in 2005. It was designed to address the limitations of earlier version control systems and enable faster, more efficient development, especially for large and distributed teams.

At its core, Git provides a way to track changes in the source code across multiple versions, making it easier to collaborate with others, maintain a clean and stable codebase, and manage code during all stages of the software development lifecycle.

Key Features of Git:

- **Distributed nature:** Unlike traditional version control systems (VCS), Git is a distributed system. Each developer's local copy of the repository is a full-fledged repository with a complete history of all changes. This allows developers to work offline and commit changes locally before syncing with the central repository.

- **Efficiency:** Git is known for its speed and scalability, handling large codebases and repositories without significant performance issues. Its operations, such as branching and merging, are fast, even with large numbers of files and commits.

- **Branching and Merging:** One of Git's key strengths is its branching model. Developers can create and switch between multiple branches easily, experiment with new features, and merge changes back into the main branch seamlessly. This allows for cleaner and more controlled development workflows.

- **Data Integrity:** Git ensures that every commit is cryptographically secure, meaning it is virtually impossible to alter any part of the repository history without being detected. This ensures the integrity of the version history.

- **Collaborative:** Git is designed for collaboration. It allows developers to clone a project, work on their changes independently, and later merge their work back into the main repository, making it an ideal tool for distributed teams working on the same project.

Git's importance cannot be overstated, especially in modern development environments. It's the tool that allows developers to manage code in teams, automate deployments, integrate with continuous integration systems, and support scalable, agile workflows.

Git vs. Other Version Control Systems (SVN, Mercurial)

While Git is the most popular version control system today, it wasn't the first. A number of other systems, like Subversion (SVN) and Mercurial, predate Git and still remain in use in some environments. Understanding how Git differs from these systems is important in appreciating its advantages.

1. Git vs. Subversion (SVN)

Subversion (SVN) is a centralized version control system (CVCS). In SVN, the entire history of the repository is stored on a central server, and developers pull down the latest changes from that central server to their local machine. While SVN was a significant improvement over older VCS systems, it has some limitations compared to Git:

- **Centralized vs. Distributed:** In SVN, developers work with a single central repository. This means that developers must be connected to the server to commit changes or fetch updates. Git, on the other hand, is distributed, and each developer has a full copy of the repository, allowing for offline work.

- **Branching:** In SVN, branching is possible but less efficient. Branching in SVN is essentially creating a copy of the directory structure, which can result in large overheads. Git's lightweight and fast branching model is one of its most powerful features.

- **Speed:** Git is generally faster than SVN, especially for common operations like committing changes, branching, and merging.

2. Git vs. Mercurial

Mercurial (Hg) is another distributed version control system, similar to Git. Both Git and Mercurial allow for offline work, but there are some differences in terms of usage and functionality:

- **Performance:** Git is typically faster than Mercurial, especially when dealing with large repositories. Git's handling of large binary files, in particular, is more efficient.

- **Popularity:** Git has become the industry standard for version control, with widespread adoption among open-source projects and major corporations. Mercurial, while still in use, has not achieved the same level of adoption.

- **Usability:** Some developers argue that Mercurial is easier to use than Git due to its simpler command set, but this simplicity often comes at the cost of flexibility. Git's extensive features and flexibility offer more power at the cost of a steeper learning curve.

In summary, while systems like SVN and Mercurial have their place in version control, Git's combination of speed, distributed architecture, and extensive support for branching and merging has made it the preferred choice for modern software development.

How Git Simplifies Collaboration in Development

Git's design makes it particularly well-suited for collaboration among developers, both within teams and across large, distributed communities. Here's how it simplifies collaboration:

1. Branching and Merging: Git's branching and merging capabilities allow multiple developers to work on the same codebase without stepping on each other's toes. Each developer can create a separate branch for their feature or bug fix, work on it independently, and merge it back into the main branch once it's complete. This means that teams can work in parallel, without worrying about code conflicts until the point of merging.

2. Distributed Nature: Git allows developers to clone the entire repository, including its history, to their local machines. This means that developers can work offline, make commits, and experiment freely, and only need an internet connection when it's time to push their changes to the central repository. This flexibility is critical for large teams that may not always be working in the same geographic location or during the same hours.

3. Pull Requests and Code Reviews: GitHub, GitLab, and other platforms built on top of Git provide powerful collaboration tools such as pull requests (PRs). A PR is a request to merge one branch into another, and it typically includes a code review process where other developers review the changes before they are merged. This ensures code quality, catches bugs early, and facilitates better communication across the team.

4. Version History and Collaboration Transparency: With Git, every change made to the repository is tracked in the commit history. Each commit includes details about what changed and who made the change. This transparency makes it easier to trace problems, understand the context of changes, and revert back to previous versions if necessary.

5. Conflict Resolution: While Git makes collaboration much smoother, conflicts can still occur when two developers make incompatible changes to the same piece of code. Git offers several tools to handle conflicts during merging. It allows developers to view, compare, and resolve conflicts manually, ensuring that the best solution is implemented.

In conclusion, Git's distributed nature, efficient branching, and merging features make it an ideal tool for collaboration in both small teams and large-scale open-source projects. It simplifies coordination, reduces the risk of conflicts, and helps developers maintain high-quality, stable codebases.

In this chapter, we've explored the need for version control, the key features and advantages of Git, how it compares to other systems like SVN and Mercurial, and how Git simplifies collaboration in software development. Understanding these fundamentals will provide you with a strong foundation for the more advanced topics covered in the rest of this book. As we continue, we'll dive deeper into the core Git commands, workflows, and best practices that make Git an essential tool for modern

CHAPTER 2: GETTING STARTED WITH GIT

Git is a powerful version control system that helps developers manage and track changes to their codebase. In this chapter, we will cover the basics of getting started with Git, including installing Git, understanding the Git file system, and running your first Git commands. By the end of this chapter, you will have a solid foundation in setting up Git and configuring it for your development environment.

Installing Git and Setting Up Your Environment

Before you can begin using Git, you need to install it on your machine. Fortunately, Git is cross-platform and can be easily installed on macOS, Windows, and Linux. Follow the steps for your specific operating system to install Git:

1. Installing Git on macOS:

- macOS often comes with Git pre-installed. To check if Git is installed, open your terminal and type the following:

css

git --version

If Git is already installed, you'll see the version number. If not, you can install it using Homebrew, a package manager for macOS:

brew install git

Alternatively, you can install Git by downloading the official installer from Git's website.

2. Installing Git on Windows:

- On Windows, the easiest way to install Git is by downloading the installer from Git's website. Once downloaded, simply run the installer and follow the on-screen instructions.
- During the installation process, you will be asked to choose several options, such as setting Git to use the default text

editor and selecting the appropriate terminal for Git Bash (which is highly recommended for a smooth experience).

3. Installing Git on Linux:

- On Linux, Git can usually be installed directly from your distribution's package manager:
    - For Debian-based distributions (like Ubuntu):

    sql

    ```
    sudo apt update
    sudo apt install git
    ```

    - For Red Hat-based distributions (like Fedora):

    ```
    sudo dnf install git
    ```

Once installed, you can verify the installation by running the following command in your terminal or command prompt:

css

```
git --version
```

This command will return the installed Git version, confirming that Git is properly set up on your machine.

Understanding the Git File System

Git organizes its data into a structured file system with three key areas that are crucial to understanding how Git works: the **working directory**, the **staging area**, and the **repository**. These areas define the flow of how files are added, modified, and committed in Git.

1. Working Directory: The working directory (also called the working tree) is where you do your actual work. It's the directory where your files reside on your local machine. This is the current state of the files you are editing. When you modify a file, it is only changed in the working directory at first.

2. Staging Area (Index): The staging area is a space where you can prepare files before committing them to the Git repository. When you modify files, they first exist in the working directory. To commit these changes to the repository, you need to stage them, which means moving them from the working directory to the staging area using the git add command.

The staging area allows you to select which changes you want to commit, giving you control over what is included in the next commit. You can stage multiple files or even just parts of a file, allowing for highly granular control over your commits.

3. Repository (Local Git Database): The repository is where Git stores all the information about your project, including the history of all commits, branches, and metadata. The repository is located in a hidden .git directory inside your project folder. It tracks all changes made to your project and ensures that you can revert back to any previous state.

When you run the git commit command, Git takes the changes from the staging area and stores them as a commit in the repository. The repository is where your project's entire version history is kept.

In summary:

- **Working Directory:** Where you modify your files.
- **Staging Area:** Where you prepare files to be committed.
- **Repository:** Where your project's history is stored.

First Git Command: git init

Once Git is installed and you understand the basic file system, it's time to initialize your first Git repository. This is done using the git init command, which converts a project directory into a Git repository. Let's break down the process:

Step 1: Create a New Project Directory First, create a new directory where you will store your project files. In the terminal or command prompt, run the following command:

perl

```
mkdir my-first-git-repo
cd my-first-git-repo
```

Step 2: Initialize the Git Repository Now that you're inside your project directory, you can initialize the repository by running the git init command:

csharp

```
git init
```

This command creates a new .git subdirectory in your project folder, which contains all the configuration files and the history of the repository. Once the repository is initialized, you can start using Git commands to track changes, create commits, and manage your project's version history.

Step 3: Check the Repository Status You can check the status of your Git repository at any time by running:

lua

```
git status
```

This command will show you the current state of your working directory and staging area. It will tell you which files have been modified, which are staged for commit, and which are untracked (i.e., not yet being tracked by Git).

Basic Configuration of Git (User Name, Email, Editor)

Before you start committing changes, you need to configure your Git settings. Git tracks commits by associating them with a user's name and email address. By default, Git will use a global configuration, but you can also specify repository-specific settings if needed.

1. Configuring Your User Name and Email: When you commit changes, Git will attach your name and email to each commit so that others can trace the history of the code changes. Run the following commands to set your name and email globally (for all repositories):

arduino

git config --global user.name "Your Name"
git config --global user.email "youremail@example.com"
These settings are saved in Git's global configuration file, typically located at ~/.gitconfig on Linux and macOS or C:\Users\YourName\.gitconfig on Windows.

If you want to set a different name or email for a specific repository, navigate to the repository directory and run:

arduino

git config user.name "Your Repo-Specific Name"
git config user.email "repo-specific-email@example.com"

2. Setting the Default Editor: Git needs a text editor for tasks such as writing commit messages. By default, Git uses the system's default editor, but you can change it to a text editor of your choice. To configure your preferred editor, run one of the following commands:

- For **VS Code**:

css

git config --global core.editor "code --wait"

- For **Vim**:

arduino

git config --global core.editor "vim"

- For **Sublime Text**:

arduino

git config --global core.editor "subl -n -w"

These settings will ensure that Git opens your chosen editor whenever you need to write a commit message or make other text edits within Git.

In this chapter, we introduced the foundational elements of getting started with Git. You learned how to install Git on different operating systems, set up your environment, and understand the key components of Git's file system: the working directory, the staging area, and the repository. You also ran your first Git command—git init—and configured Git with your name, email, and preferred editor.

These are the first steps to becoming proficient in using Git for version control. As you continue to explore Git, you will learn how to manage your code effectively, track changes, and collaborate with others in a seamless and organized way. In the next chapter, we'll delve into tracking changes and creating commits, which are essential parts of any development workflow.

CHAPTER 3: CREATING AND MANAGING REPOSITORIES

In this chapter, we will dive deeper into the essential actions that every developer needs to master when working with Git: creating and managing repositories. Repositories are where your project's files and version history are stored, and learning how to create and manage them is the foundation for using Git effectively. Whether you are working on a new project or collaborating on an existing one, understanding how to create and manage repositories is critical.

We will explore the following topics in this chapter:

- **Creating a new repository with git init**
- **Cloning an existing repository with git clone**
- **Working with remote repositories**

- **Basic repository management**

1. Creating a New Repository with git init

The first step in managing a project with Git is creating a repository. The simplest way to create a new Git repository is by using the git init command. When you run this command, Git will initialize an empty repository in the current directory, creating a .git directory that contains all the information needed to track and manage your project.

Step 1: Create a New Directory (Optional)

If you're starting from scratch and don't yet have a project folder, first create a new directory for your project:

perl

```
mkdir my-project
cd my-project
```

Step 2: Initialize the Repository

Once you are inside your project folder, you can initialize a Git repository by running:

csharp

```
git init
```

This creates a new .git directory, where Git will store all its data about the repository. The repository is now initialized, and Git is ready to track changes in the files within the project.

Step 3: Check the Repository Status

After initializing the repository, you can use git status to confirm that Git is tracking the folder:

lua

git status

At this point, Git will tell you that you have an untracked file (if there are files in the directory) or that the directory is empty.

Step 4: Add and Commit Files

You can now start adding files to your repository. To add files to the staging area, use the git add command:

csharp

git add filename.txt

Once files are staged, commit them to the repository:

sql

git commit -m "Initial commit"

With this, you've created a new repository and committed the first changes to it!

2. *Cloning an Existing Repository with git clone*

If you want to contribute to an existing project or simply work on someone else's code, you will need to clone the repository to your local machine. Cloning is the process of copying a remote repository to your local machine, so you can work with it just like you would with a locally initialized repository.

Step 1: Find the Repository URL

First, you need to find the URL of the repository you want to clone. This could be from a public repository on GitHub, GitLab, Bitbucket, or any other Git hosting service. Typically, you'll see a green "Code" button on the repository page that provides a URL for cloning. There are two main URL types:

- HTTPS: https://github.com/user/repository.git
- SSH: git@github.com:user/repository.git

Step 2: Clone the Repository

Once you have the repository URL, use the git clone command to clone the repository:

bash

git clone https://github.com/user/repository.git

or if you are using SSH:

bash

git clone git@github.com:user/repository.git

This command creates a copy of the remote repository on your local machine. It also automatically sets up a reference to the original repository as the remote called origin. You now have a full copy of the project, including its commit history.

Step 3: Navigate to the Cloned Repository

Once the clone operation is complete, navigate into the project directory:

bash

cd repository

From here, you can start working with the repository just like any other local Git repository. You can modify files, create branches, stage changes, commit them, and push them back to the remote repository.

3. Working with Remote Repositories

A significant part of Git's power comes from its ability to interact with remote repositories, which are often hosted on services like GitHub, GitLab, or Bitbucket. These remote repositories allow multiple developers to collaborate on the same project, and understanding how to manage them is essential for working in a team.

Git provides several commands for working with remote repositories, such as git remote, git fetch, git pull, and git push.

1. Adding a Remote Repository

When you initialize a new repository or clone an existing one, you can link it to a remote repository. A remote repository is simply a version of the repository that is hosted on a server, allowing for collaboration.

- To add a remote repository to your project, use the git remote add command:

  csharp

  git remote add origin https://github.com/user/repository.git

  Here, origin is the default name for the remote repository. This command tells Git to connect your local repository to the remote repository specified by the URL.

2. Fetching Changes from the Remote Repository

If other people are contributing to a project, you'll want to keep your local repository up to date with the remote repository. You can use git fetch to retrieve any changes from the remote repository without merging them into your local repository:

sql

git fetch origin

This downloads any new commits from the remote repository, but it doesn't change your working directory. It just updates your local copy of the remote branch.

3. Pulling Changes from the Remote Repository

git pull is the command you use to fetch changes from the remote repository and automatically merge them into your local branch:

css

git pull origin main

This fetches the latest changes from the remote main branch and merges them with your local branch.

4. Pushing Changes to the Remote Repository

Once you have made changes locally (added, committed, and tested), you'll want to push those changes back to the remote repository so others can see them. You can push changes using:

css

git push origin main

This command uploads your local changes to the remote repository's main branch. If you're working on a feature branch, replace main with the appropriate branch name.

4. Basic Repository Management

Now that you understand how to create, clone, and work with remote repositories, let's look at some basic repository management tasks. These tasks will help you maintain your repository and ensure it's organized and collaborative-friendly.

1. Viewing the Current Remotes

You can check which remote repositories are connected to your local repository using the git remote -v command:

git remote -v

This shows the URL of the remote repositories (usually origin) for both fetch and push operations.

2. Renaming a Remote

If you need to rename a remote repository (for example, if you want to change origin to something else), you can use:

arduino

git remote rename origin new-remote-name

3. Removing a Remote

To remove a remote repository (for example, if you no longer need to push or pull from it), you can run:

arduino

git remote remove origin

4. Checking the Repository Status

At any time, you can check the current status of your repository by running:

lua

git status

This command will give you an overview of the current branch, any uncommitted changes, files staged for commit, and files that are not yet being tracked by Git.

5. Viewing Commit History

You can see the commit history of your repository with:

bash

git log

This shows a detailed history of all commits made in the repository, including commit IDs, author information, date, and commit messages.

In this chapter, we covered the essential skills for creating and managing repositories using Git. Here's a quick recap:

- **Creating a New Repository:** You can initialize a new repository in your project folder using git init.
- **Cloning a Repository:** You can clone an existing remote repository to your local machine using git clone.
- **Working with Remote Repositories:** We explored how to add a remote, fetch changes, pull updates, and push your changes to a remote repository.
- **Basic Repository Management:** We discussed commands to manage your remotes, check repository status, and view commit history.

With these skills, you're now ready to start working with repositories in Git and collaborating with others on real-world projects. In the next chapter, we will explore how to track changes, stage files, and commit them to your Git repository, an essential skill for any developer.

CHAPTER 4: BASIC GIT WORKFLOW

In this chapter, we will dive into the **basic Git workflow**, which forms the core of how developers interact with their repositories. Understanding this workflow is essential for efficient version control, and mastering it will make collaboration and project management easier and more effective.

We will cover the following:

- **Making Changes: git add, git commit**
- **Viewing the Commit History with git log**
- **Understanding Commit Messages**
- **Committing Frequently and with Clarity**

Let's walk through the workflow step by step and explore each concept in depth.

1. Making Changes: git add, git commit

The most fundamental operations in Git involve modifying your files and then saving those modifications (committing them) to the repository. Git tracks changes at the file level, and the basic process is as follows:

Step 1: Modifying Files

To start, you modify or create files in your working directory. For example, let's say you have a README.md file in your project, and you want to make changes to it. You can edit it as you would any other text file.

Step 2: Staging Changes with git add

After modifying a file, Git doesn't immediately track your changes. Before you can commit changes to the repository, you need to **stage** them. This is where the git add command comes into play.

To stage a single file, use the following command:

csharp

git add README.md

This adds the modified README.md file to the **staging area**. The staging area is like a buffer where changes wait to be committed. It allows you to review and control what changes get included in the next commit.

You can also stage multiple files at once:

csharp

git add .

This command stages all changes in the current directory and subdirectories, including new, modified, and deleted files.

Step 3: Committing Changes with git commit

Once the changes are staged, it's time to commit them. Committing is the process of saving changes to your repository, making them a permanent part of the project's history.

To commit the staged changes, use:

sql

git commit -m "Updated README with new project information"
The -m flag is followed by a **commit message**, which describes the changes you've made. Commit messages are essential for tracking project history and understanding what was done in each commit.

The commit itself will include the changes in the files that were staged with git add up to this point.

2. Viewing the Commit History with git log

Once you have started making commits, it's important to be able to view the history of your changes. Git provides the git log command to display a log of all the commits in your repository.

Basic git log Usage

To view the commit history, run:

bash

git log

By default, this will display the commits in reverse chronological order (most recent first), showing the commit hash (a unique identifier for the commit), the author, the date, and the commit message.

Here's an example output:

sql

```
commit 7d2c4321fbe0fbb5a95d8f09b5bcf14f5d37be47
Author: John Doe <john.doe@example.com>
Date:   Mon Oct 10 12:34:56 2024 -0700

    Updated README with new project information

commit b730a6821e9aeb730f4220ccf83be89c6fe5c207
Author: John Doe <john.doe@example.com>
```

Date: Sun Oct 9 14:12:22 2024 -0700

Added installation instructions to README

In the output, you can see the commit hash (like 7d2c4321fbe0fbb5a95d8f09b5bcf14f5d37be47), the author's name and email, the commit date, and the commit message.

Customizing git log Output

Git's log command has several options to customize its output. For example:

- To limit the number of commits shown, use:

bash

git log -n 5

This shows the last 5 commits.

- To display the log with more concise information (commit hash and message), use:

lua

git log --oneline

This will display each commit on a single line, making it easier to read a high-level overview of the project history.

vbnet

7d2c432 Updated README with new project information
b730a68 Added installation instructions to README

3. Understanding Commit Messages

Commit messages are essential for keeping track of the changes in a repository. A good commit message explains **why** a change was made, not just **what** was changed. A good commit message follows a clear, readable format and helps other developers (or even your future self) understand the reasoning behind changes without having to look at the code.

The Structure of a Good Commit Message

A standard commit message consists of three parts:

1. **Subject Line** (short summary of the change)
2. **Body** (optional; a more detailed explanation of why the change was made)
3. **Footer** (optional; for references to issues or pull requests)

Here's an example of a well-structured commit message:

css

Add feature to allow users to reset passwords

This commit adds a "Forgot Password" button to the login page. When clicked,

users will be prompted to enter their email address, and a reset link will be

sent to their inbox. This feature improves security and user experience.

Closes #123

- The **subject line** is brief, no more than 50 characters, and written in the present tense.
- The **body** provides further explanation of the change, especially if it involves a more complex update.
- The **footer** references an issue number or pull request ID, if applicable.

Why Commit Messages Matter

- **Documentation:** Commit messages serve as documentation for the changes made to the repository.
- **Collaboration:** Clear messages make it easier for team members to understand the changes and make informed decisions about code reviews.

- **History:** Well-written commit messages help preserve the context of decisions for future reference, making it easier to understand the evolution of the project.

4. Committing Frequently and with Clarity

One of the key principles of version control is committing often. Committing frequently allows you to:

- **Track incremental changes:** By committing frequently, you create small, logical chunks of work. This makes it easier to track progress, locate bugs, and roll back to a previous state if needed.
- **Avoid large, unmanageable commits:** If you wait too long to commit, your commit might end up being too large, making it difficult to review, understand, or merge.
- **Reduce conflicts:** Frequent commits ensure that changes are integrated regularly, reducing the likelihood of conflicts when collaborating with others.

Best Practices for Committing Frequently

- **Commit early and often:** As soon as you make a logical change, commit it. Don't wait until the end of the day or after finishing a large feature.

- **Commit small, focused changes:** Each commit should focus on a single change or fix. For example, don't commit unrelated changes (e.g., adding a feature and fixing a typo in one commit).

- **Use meaningful commit messages:** Follow the best practices for writing commit messages, ensuring that the message describes both **what** was changed and **why**.

Avoiding "WIP" (Work-in-Progress) Commits

While it might be tempting to make a commit just to save your work (e.g., with a message like "WIP"), this practice should be avoided. Instead, aim for commits that clearly describe the completed portion of work. If you need to save your progress without committing, use git stash to temporarily store your changes without committing them.

In this chapter, we've covered the basic Git workflow that every developer should understand. We explored the following steps:

1. **Making Changes:** You modify files and then use git add to stage the changes and git commit to save them to the repository.

2. **Viewing the Commit History:** You can use git log to view the commit history and track the evolution of your project.

3. **Understanding Commit Messages:** A good commit message explains what changed and why, making the project history clearer for you and others.

4. **Committing Frequently and with Clarity:** Committing often with clear messages ensures that your changes are well-documented, manageable, and easy to collaborate on.

By mastering these basic Git commands, you'll be able to manage your repository more efficiently and lay a strong foundation for more advanced Git concepts in future chapters.

CHAPTER 5: BRANCHING BASICS

Branching is one of the core concepts in Git that makes it incredibly powerful, allowing you to work on multiple versions of a project simultaneously. In this chapter, we'll dive into the fundamentals of Git branches, explaining their purpose, how to create and switch between them, and how to merge changes from different branches. We'll also cover how to resolve conflicts that can arise during merging.

We will cover the following:

- **What are branches in Git?**
- **Creating and switching branches with git branch and git checkout**
- **Merging branches with git merge**

- **Resolving conflicts in merges**

1. What Are Branches in Git?

In Git, a **branch** is essentially a lightweight pointer to a specific commit in your repository. By default, Git starts you off with a single branch, called master (or main in more recent Git versions), which holds the history of your project. However, as development progresses, you'll often need to create new branches to work on features, bug fixes, or experiments without disturbing the main line of development.

Think of a branch as a separate timeline for your project. You can make changes, commit them, and merge them back into the main project once the work is complete and stable.

Why Use Branches?

- **Parallel Development:** Branches allow developers to work on different tasks without interfering with each other. For example, one developer could be working on a feature, while another works on a bug fix.
- **Feature Isolation:** By using branches, you can isolate features or bug fixes, allowing you to work on them independently of the main codebase. This makes it easier to

experiment with new ideas or make changes without affecting production code.

- **Collaboration:** Branching is essential when multiple developers are working on the same project. It helps prevent conflicts because each developer can work in their own branch and later merge their changes into the main branch.

Default Branches

- **Master/Main:** The main branch, where the stable, production-ready code lives.
- **Feature Branches:** Branches created to develop specific features or bug fixes.
- **Release Branches:** Created when you're preparing for a new release.
- **Hotfix Branches:** Used to quickly patch bugs in the production environment.

2. Creating and Switching Branches with git branch and git checkout

Creating a Branch

To create a new branch, you use the git branch command followed by the name of the branch you want to create. For example, to create a branch called feature-login, run the following command:

git branch feature-login

This command will create a new branch called feature-login, but it does not switch to it. The new branch is created based on the current branch you're on.

Switching Between Branches

After creating a new branch, you need to switch to it in order to start working on it. You can switch between branches using the git checkout command.

To switch to the newly created feature-login branch:

git checkout feature-login

After switching, your working directory will be updated to reflect the state of the feature-login branch.

Creating and Switching in One Step

You can also combine the creation of a branch and switching to it into a single command by using:

css

git checkout -b feature-login

This command will create the branch feature-login and immediately switch to it.

Listing All Branches

To view all the branches in your repository, use:

git branch

This will list all branches, and the current branch will be highlighted with an asterisk (*). For example:

css

```
* main
  feature-login
  feature-search
```

3. Merging Branches with git merge

Once you've completed work in a feature branch, you often need to bring those changes back into the main branch (usually main or master). This is done through a **merge**. The git merge command combines the changes from one branch into another.

How Merging Works

To merge a branch, first make sure you're on the branch that you want to merge changes into. For example, if you're on the main branch and want to merge the changes from feature-login, you would run:

css

```
git checkout main
git merge feature-login
```

This process brings all the commits from feature-login into main. If there are no conflicts, Git will automatically fast-forward and add the changes. A commit is created for the merge to record that the two branches were combined.

Fast-Forward Merges

A fast-forward merge happens when there is a direct path from the current branch to the branch you're merging. In this case, Git simply moves the pointer of the target branch forward to the latest commit of the source branch. This is the simplest type of merge and occurs when no other commits have been made on the target branch since the branching point.

Example:

css

```
git checkout main
```

git merge feature-login

In this case, Git will just update main to the latest commit from feature-login because there were no changes on main since the branch point.

Merge Commit

In cases where both branches have diverged (i.e., both have commits since the branch was created), Git will create a **merge commit** that brings together both sets of changes.

This is done by creating a new commit that has two parents: one from the main branch and one from the feature-login branch. The merge commit will include the changes from both branches, preserving the history of both.

4. Resolving Conflicts in Merges

While merging is a simple operation in many cases, conflicts can occur when changes in two branches touch the same part of a file. A **merge conflict** happens when Git cannot automatically reconcile differences between two sets of changes. For example, if both the main and feature-login branches have changes to the same line in a file, Git will not know which version to keep.

How Git Handles Merge Conflicts

When a conflict occurs, Git will mark the conflicted areas in the file and prevent the merge from completing. It's up to the developer to manually resolve the conflict.

Here's an example of what a conflict might look like in a file:

python

```
<<<<<<< HEAD
print("Hello from main branch")
=======
print("Hello from feature-login branch")
>>>>>>> feature-login
```

In this example, the two branches have different print() statements, and Git doesn't know which one to keep. The markers <<<<<<<, =======, and >>>>>>> indicate the conflicting changes, where:

- HEAD represents the current branch (in this case, main).
- The part after ======= represents the changes from the branch being merged (in this case, feature-login).

Resolving Conflicts

To resolve a merge conflict:

1. Open the conflicted file in a text editor.
2. Look for the conflict markers (<<<<<<<, =======, >>>>>>>), and decide which changes to keep.

3. Remove the conflict markers after deciding what changes to retain, and make the file reflect the final desired result.

Once the conflict is resolved:

csharp

```
git add <filename>
```

This stages the resolved file. After all conflicts are resolved and staged, you can complete the merge:

sql

```
git commit
```

Git will create a merge commit, and the merge process will be complete.

Best Practices for Avoiding Merge Conflicts

- **Commit frequently and early:** The more frequently you commit and merge changes, the less likely you are to encounter complex conflicts.
- **Communicate with your team:** Regularly pull the latest changes from the main branch to keep your branch up to date and avoid conflicts down the road.

- **Use feature branches:** Always work on feature branches, and try to keep them as focused as possible on a single task or change.

In this chapter, we covered the basics of **branching** in Git, which is a critical aspect of effective version control. Key topics included:

1. **What Are Branches in Git?**: Branches provide a way to isolate different tasks and make parallel development easier.

2. **Creating and Switching Branches**: You learned how to create and switch between branches using git branch and git checkout.

3. **Merging Branches**: We explored how to bring changes from one branch into another using git merge, including fast-forward merges and merge commits.

4. **Resolving Merge Conflicts**: We discussed how conflicts can arise during merges, and the steps you can take to resolve them manually.

Mastering branching and merging is essential for effective collaboration and project management in Git. These skills will enable you to work on features independently, integrate changes seamlessly, and manage complex project histories efficiently. As you continue working with Git, understanding how branches function and how to resolve conflicts will become second nature, allowing you to focus more on development and less on managing your code.

CHAPTER 6: REMOTE REPOSITORIES: INTRODUCTION TO GITHUB

As we continue to explore the capabilities of Git, one of the most powerful features is its ability to work with **remote repositories**.

These repositories, typically hosted on platforms like GitHub, GitLab, or Bitbucket, allow developers to collaborate, share code, and maintain version control over a distributed network. In this chapter, we will explore **GitHub**, one of the most popular platforms for hosting remote Git repositories, and discuss how it integrates seamlessly with Git. We'll cover setting up a GitHub account, connecting local repositories to GitHub, and using commands like git push and git pull to push and pull changes between your local and remote repositories.

We'll cover the following topics:

- **What is GitHub and how it integrates with Git**
- **Creating a GitHub account**
- **Connecting local repositories to GitHub**
- **Pushing and pulling changes with git push and git pull**

1. What is GitHub and How It Integrates with Git?

GitHub is a cloud-based platform that hosts Git repositories. It is used by millions of developers and teams to collaborate on projects. GitHub offers several features on top of Git, such as pull requests, issue tracking, and collaboration tools, making it a more powerful and user-friendly platform for version control. GitHub is built on Git, meaning that it takes full advantage of Git's capabilities while adding additional tools for social coding and collaboration.

Git vs GitHub

While **Git** is the underlying version control system, **GitHub** is a web-based service that hosts Git repositories. Here are the key differences:

- **Git** is the tool that tracks and manages changes to files locally on your computer. It is a version control system that allows you to create, manage, and merge different versions of your project.
- **GitHub** is a hosting platform that allows you to share your Git repositories online, collaborate with others, and integrate with a range of additional services.

Think of Git as the engine of version control, and GitHub as the platform that hosts the repositories and adds features to enhance collaboration. When you push your local Git repository to GitHub, you make your project accessible to others, enabling easy sharing, collaboration, and version tracking in the cloud.

Key Features of GitHub

- **Forking**: You can create a personal copy of someone else's repository to make changes independently.
- **Pull Requests**: A way of proposing changes to a repository. After making changes in your forked repository, you can open a pull request to ask the original project to incorporate your changes.

- **Issues**: A way to track bugs, tasks, and enhancements in a repository.
- **Actions**: Automated workflows that can be set up to run tests, deploy code, or handle other CI/CD tasks.
- **GitHub Pages**: A feature that lets you host static websites directly from a GitHub repository.

GitHub is not the only platform for hosting Git repositories, but it is by far the most popular and widely used in the developer community, especially for open-source projects.

2. Creating a GitHub Account

Before you can connect a local Git repository to GitHub, you need to create an account. Here's how you can do that:

Step 1: Go to GitHub

1. Open your browser and go to https://github.com.
2. If you don't already have an account, click **Sign up** in the upper-right corner.
3. You will be prompted to enter a username, email address, and password.
4. Follow the on-screen instructions to verify your email address and complete the account creation process.

Step 2: Choose a Plan

GitHub offers several plans:

- **Free**: Public repositories and limited private repositories.
- **Pro**: More private repositories, advanced features for individuals.
- **Team**: Collaboration tools for teams and organizations.
- **Enterprise**: A fully managed GitHub solution for large organizations.

For most personal and small-scale projects, the free plan is sufficient, which includes unlimited public and private repositories with up to three collaborators.

Step 3: Customize Your GitHub Profile

Once your account is created, you can add more details to your profile:

- **Profile Picture**: Upload a profile picture to help others recognize you.
- **Bio**: Add a short bio about yourself.
- **Social Links**: Link to your personal website, Twitter, LinkedIn, or other social media accounts.

Now you're ready to start working with GitHub!

3. Connecting Local Repositories to GitHub

To connect your local Git repository to GitHub, you need to create a repository on GitHub and then link it to your local project.

Step 1: Create a New Repository on GitHub

1. Once you're logged into GitHub, click the + icon in the upper-right corner of the page.
2. Select **New repository** from the dropdown menu.
3. Give your repository a name (e.g., my-awesome-project).
4. Optionally, add a description and choose whether the repository will be **public** or **private**.
5. Click **Create repository** to create the repository on GitHub.

GitHub will then display a page with instructions on how to connect your local repository to this new GitHub repository. These instructions will look something like this:

bash

```
# Create a new repository on your local machine
git init


# Add files and make your first commit
git add .
git commit -m "Initial commit"


# Add the GitHub repository as a remote
```

```
git remote add origin https://github.com/yourusername/my-
awesome-project.git
```

Push the changes to GitHub
```
git push -u origin master
```

Step 2: Add the Remote Repository to Your Local Git Repository

To link your local repository to GitHub, use the git remote add command. This tells Git where your remote repository (i.e., GitHub repository) is located.

bash

```
git remote add origin https://github.com/yourusername/my-
awesome-project.git
```

This command establishes a connection between your local repository and the remote repository on GitHub. You can check if the remote has been added by running:

bash

```
git remote -v
```

You should see something like:

perl

origin   https://github.com/yourusername/my-awesome-project.git (fetch)

origin   https://github.com/yourusername/my-awesome-project.git (push)

4. Pushing and Pulling Changes with git push and git pull

Once your local repository is connected to GitHub, you can start pushing and pulling changes between your local machine and the GitHub repository.

Pushing Changes to GitHub (git push)

The git push command uploads your commits from your local repository to the remote repository on GitHub. This is how you share your changes with others and make them available online.

To push your changes to GitHub, use the following command:

bash

git push origin master
In this command:

- origin is the default name for your remote repository (which we set earlier).
- master is the name of the branch you are pushing to (in this case, master or main).

If you're pushing to a branch other than master (e.g., feature-login), you can specify the branch name:

bash

git push origin feature-login

Pulling Changes from GitHub (git pull)

The git pull command retrieves changes from the remote repository and integrates them into your local repository. This is especially useful for collaborating with others, as it allows you to stay up to date with the latest changes made to the remote repository.

To pull changes from GitHub, use:

bash

git pull origin master

This command fetches the latest changes from the master branch of the remote repository and merges them into your current branch.

Resolving Conflicts During Pull

If someone else has made changes to the same lines of code that you've also modified, a conflict will occur when you run git pull. Git will inform you that there is a conflict and require you to resolve it manually. You can use the conflict resolution methods mentioned in the **Branching Basics** chapter to resolve any issues.

In this chapter, we explored **GitHub**—the leading platform for hosting Git repositories—and how it integrates with Git to provide a robust solution for managing and collaborating on software projects. We covered the following key points:

- **What is GitHub?**: GitHub is a platform for hosting Git repositories, offering additional features for collaboration and version control.
- **Creating a GitHub Account**: Step-by-step instructions for setting up a GitHub account.
- **Connecting Local Repositories to GitHub**: How to link your local Git repository with a GitHub repository using git remote add and git push.
- **Pushing and Pulling Changes**: The commands git push and git pull to upload and download changes between your local machine and GitHub.

Mastering these concepts will allow you to collaborate efficiently with other developers and keep your project synchronized across multiple machines. GitHub, along with Git, is an indispensable tool for modern software development.

CHAPTER 7: COLLABORATION USING GITHUB

One of the core strengths of Git and GitHub is the ability to facilitate collaboration among multiple developers, teams, and even organizations. GitHub provides a suite of tools that make it easy to contribute to projects, whether you're working within a team or contributing to open-source software. In this chapter, we'll cover the essential GitHub collaboration features, including **cloning repositories**, **forking repositories**, **working with pull requests (PRs)**, and **reviewing and merging PRs**. We will also discuss **best practices** for collaborating on GitHub to ensure a smooth and productive development process.

1. Cloning Repositories from GitHub

Before you can contribute to a project on GitHub, you typically need to get a copy of the repository onto your local machine. This is done using the git clone command.

What is Cloning?

Cloning a repository means making an exact copy of a repository from GitHub (or another remote) onto your local machine. This allows you to start working on the project locally without affecting the original repository. Cloning is typically used when you're either starting a new feature, fixing a bug, or reviewing code in an existing project.

Steps to Clone a Repository

1. **Find the Repository on GitHub**: Navigate to the repository you want to clone on GitHub.

2. **Copy the Repository URL**: In the top-right corner of the repository page, click on the green **Code** button and copy the URL. This could either be an HTTPS or SSH URL. For example:

   o HTTPS: https://github.com/username/repository.git

   o SSH: git@github.com:username/repository.git (SSH is often used for security reasons and avoids entering credentials repeatedly).

3. **Clone the Repository**: Open your terminal and navigate to the directory where you want to clone the repository. Run the following command:

bash

git clone https://github.com/username/repository.git
After this, Git will download a full copy of the repository (including all files and commit history) to your local machine.

4. **Navigate to the Project Directory**: Once cloning is complete, you can enter the repository's directory:

bash

cd repository
Now, you can begin working with the code locally.

2. Forking Repositories

When you want to contribute to a project but don't have write access to the original repository (such as contributing to open-source software), you need to **fork** the repository. Forking creates a personal copy of the repository under your GitHub account, where you can freely make changes without affecting the original project.

What is Forking?

Forking a repository means creating a copy of the repository on your GitHub account. You can then make changes to this copy, and when you're ready, you can propose those changes back to the original repository through a pull request.

Steps to Fork a Repository

1. **Go to the Repository on GitHub**: Find the repository you want to fork.
2. **Click on the Fork Button**: In the upper-right corner of the repository page, click on the **Fork** button. GitHub will create a copy of the repository under your account.
3. **Clone the Forked Repository**: Once the repository has been forked, you can clone it to your local machine using

the same steps as you would for cloning any repository. The URL will be something like:

bash

git clone https://github.com/yourusername/repository.git

4. **Start Working on Your Fork**: You can now work on your forked copy of the repository, making changes and committing them as needed.

3. Working with Pull Requests (PRs)

A **pull request (PR)** is the mechanism by which you propose changes to the original repository (or to another branch within the same repository). After making changes in your local repository or forked repository, you can open a pull request to merge those changes into the original repository.

What is a Pull Request?

A **pull request** is a request to merge changes you've made (in a feature branch or fork) into another branch (often the main or master branch) of the original repository. Pull requests allow maintainers to review changes before they are merged, ensuring the changes align with the project's goals and standards.

Steps to Create a Pull Request

1. **Push Your Changes to GitHub**: After making changes in your local repository, you need to push them to your forked repository on GitHub. Run:

   bash

   git push origin your-branch-name

2. **Open a Pull Request**: Go to your forked repository on GitHub and click on the **Compare & pull request** button that GitHub suggests after you push your changes.

3. **Provide a Descriptive Title and Comment**: In the pull request page, give your PR a descriptive title that summarizes the changes you made. In the comment box, provide a detailed description of the changes, why you made them, and any additional context that might help the reviewer.

4. **Select the Base and Compare Branches**: GitHub allows you to compare branches from your fork with the original repository. In most cases, the base branch will be the main or master branch of the original repository. You'll be comparing your branch (which contains the changes) with the base branch.

5. **Create the Pull Request**: Once you've filled in all the information, click the **Create pull request** button to submit it.

4. Reviewing and Merging Pull Requests

Once a pull request has been submitted, the repository maintainers or other collaborators can review your changes. During this process, they might leave comments, ask for changes, or approve the request.

Reviewing Pull Requests

When reviewing a pull request, the reviewer will typically look for:

- **Code Quality**: Is the code well-written, clean, and follows the project's coding standards?
- **Functionality**: Does the code do what it's supposed to do? Are there any bugs?
- **Testing**: Are there tests to verify that the code works correctly?
- **Documentation**: Is the code properly documented, and are the commit messages clear and meaningful?

Reviewers can leave comments directly on the lines of code in the pull request, suggesting changes or asking questions. They can also approve or request changes to the pull request.

Merging Pull Requests

Once the pull request is approved, it can be merged into the base branch of the repository. This is typically done by the repository maintainer or the person who created the pull request if they have the necessary permissions.

To merge a pull request, the reviewer or repository maintainer can:

1. Click on the **Merge pull request** button.
2. Optionally, edit the commit message for the merge.
3. Confirm the merge by clicking **Confirm merge**.

Once merged, the changes are incorporated into the base branch, and the pull request is closed.

Deleting a Branch After Merging

After a pull request has been merged, it's considered good practice to delete the feature branch (unless you plan to use it for further work). This keeps the repository clean and reduces clutter.

On GitHub, you'll often see a **Delete branch** button after merging a pull request. You can click it to remove the branch, or you can do it manually using:

bash

```
git branch -d your-branch-name
```

5. Best Practices for Collaboration

When collaborating on a project with others, following certain best practices ensures smooth workflows, reduces confusion, and leads to higher-quality contributions. Below are a few key best practices for collaborating using Git and GitHub.

a. Commit Frequently and with Descriptive Messages

- **Commit often**: Commit your changes frequently to keep your work organized and minimize merge conflicts.
- **Write clear commit messages**: Each commit message should be descriptive and explain the reasoning behind the change. A good commit message format is:
    - **Short (50 characters or less)**: A concise description of the change.
    - **Body (optional)**: A detailed explanation of the change, why it was made, and any context or caveats.

b. Use Feature Branches

- **Create feature branches**: Always work on a separate branch for each feature or bug fix, rather than directly on the main or master branch. This keeps your work organized and makes it easier to collaborate.

    Example:

bash

git checkout -b feature-new-login

c. Keep Pull Requests Focused

- **Limit the scope of each pull request**: Each pull request should focus on a single task or feature. This makes it easier for reviewers to understand the change and provide feedback.
- **Avoid large PRs**: Large pull requests can be difficult to review. Try to break changes down into smaller, more manageable pieces.

d. Communicate with Team Members

- **Use issues and labels**: GitHub issues are a great way to track bugs, feature requests, and discussions. Use labels to categorize issues and keep track of their status.
- **Discuss changes in pull requests**: If you're not sure about a change, ask for feedback directly in the pull request comments.

e. Stay Updated with git pull

- **Pull frequently**: If you're working in a team, run git pull often to keep your local repository up to date with the latest changes from your teammates. This reduces the chances of conflicts when you push your changes.

f. Use Continuous Integration/Continuous Deployment (CI/CD)

- **Set up CI/CD**: Automate testing, building, and deployment using CI/CD tools like GitHub Actions. This ensures that code changes are automatically tested and deployed, making the process smoother and more reliable.

In this chapter, we've covered the basic workflows of **cloning**, **forking**, **working with pull requests**, and **merging** changes, along with the best practices for collaborating on GitHub. By following these workflows and practices, you can contribute to projects efficiently, ensure your changes are reviewed properly, and maintain a smooth collaboration experience with your team.

CHAPTER 8: ADVANCED BRANCHING TECHNIQUES

Branching is one of the most powerful features of Git. It allows developers to work on multiple versions of a project simultaneously, without affecting the main codebase. As you become more experienced with Git, you'll need to understand advanced branching techniques to handle complex workflows and maintain a streamlined development process.

In this chapter, we'll dive deep into advanced branching techniques, including:

- **Understanding merge vs. rebase**
- **Handling long-lived branches**
- **Creating and managing feature branches**
- **Using Git Flow and other branching strategies**

By the end of this chapter, you'll have a strong understanding of how to manage complex branching scenarios and apply the best practices for effective collaboration and project management.

1. Understanding Merge vs. Rebase

When working with branches in Git, you'll encounter two fundamental ways to combine changes from one branch into another: **merge** and **rebase**. Both of these techniques allow you to integrate changes from different branches, but they do so in different ways, with different effects on your commit history.

Merge

The git merge command is the most commonly used method for integrating changes from one branch into another. It combines the histories of the two branches, creating a new merge commit in the target branch.

How git merge works:

1. You have two branches: main and feature-branch.
2. The feature-branch contains several commits that need to be merged into main.
3. You switch to the main branch and run git merge feature-branch.

   bash

   ```
   git checkout main
   git merge feature-branch
   ```

4. Git will attempt to combine the changes automatically. If there are no conflicts, a merge commit is created on the main branch, and both histories are preserved.

Advantages of git merge:

- **Non-destructive**: git merge preserves the full history of both branches. It keeps the commit history as it was, with no changes to the existing commits.

- **Clear commit history**: The merge commit explicitly marks the point where the branches were combined, making it easy to track the history of merges.

Disadvantages of git merge:

- **Complex history**: If you frequently merge branches, your commit history can become cluttered with a series of merge commits, making it harder to follow the project's development timeline.

Rebase

The git rebase command is another method for integrating changes between branches, but it works differently. Instead of creating a merge commit, git rebase moves or "reapplies" the changes from one branch onto another, effectively rewriting the commit history.

How git rebase works:

1. You have the same two branches: main and feature-branch.
2. The feature-branch contains several commits that need to be applied to main.
3. You switch to the feature-branch and run git rebase main.

bash

```
git checkout feature-branch
```

git rebase main

4. Git will take the commits from feature-branch, replay them on top of the latest commit of the main branch, and update the feature-branch to reflect those changes. This makes it appear as though the changes on feature-branch were made after the latest commit on main.

Advantages of git rebase:

- **Clean commit history**: Rebasing creates a linear commit history, which makes the project's history easier to understand. This is especially useful for feature branches and small teams.
- **No merge commits**: Rebasing avoids the creation of merge commits, keeping the history simpler and cleaner.

Disadvantages of git rebase:

- **Destructive**: Since rebase rewrites commit history, it's more dangerous than merging, especially when working with shared branches. If you rebase commits that have already been pushed to a remote repository, you can create conflicts for other collaborators.
- **Requires caution**: It's essential to be cautious when rebasing shared branches, as it can cause confusion and difficult-to-resolve conflicts.

When to Use Merge vs. Rebase

- Use **merge** when:
  - o You want to preserve the full commit history of both branches.
  - o You are merging long-lived branches or feature branches that have already been shared with others.
  - o You want a clear visual marker for the point at which branches were integrated.
- Use **rebase** when:
  - o You want a clean, linear commit history.
  - o You are working on a feature branch and need to incorporate the latest changes from main before merging your changes.
  - o You are working alone or in a small team and are confident that your rebasing won't affect others.

2. Handling Long-Lived Branches

Long-lived branches are branches that exist for an extended period of time, such as the main or develop branches in large projects. They are often used for stable code that reflects the current state of the project.

Challenges with Long-Lived Branches:

- **Divergence**: Over time, long-lived branches tend to diverge, and the longer the branch exists, the more potential there is for conflicts when merging.
- **Integration complexity**: When you have multiple developers working on long-lived branches, you may face complex merges or rebasing conflicts as various features and bug fixes are integrated.

Best Practices for Managing Long-Lived Branches:

1. **Frequent Merges or Rebases**: To minimize divergence, regularly merge changes from main or develop into your long-lived branch. Alternatively, you can rebase your long-lived branch onto the latest version of main or develop to keep it up-to-date.

   bash

   ```
   git checkout feature-branch
   git merge main
   ```

2. **Modularize Your Work**: If you're working on a large feature, break it into smaller, manageable sub-features. This makes it easier to integrate changes into long-lived branches without causing massive merge conflicts.

3. **Use Pull Requests for Long-Lived Branches**: For large changes, it's essential to use pull requests to ensure

thorough code reviews and discussions before merging into long-lived branches.

4. **Test Often**: Continuously test your code to ensure it works as expected when merged into the long-lived branch. Use automated testing pipelines if available.

3. Creating and Managing Feature Branches

Feature branches are temporary branches that are used to work on specific features or tasks. They are an essential part of collaborative development workflows, as they allow developers to isolate their work until it is ready to be integrated into the main codebase.

Creating a Feature Branch:

Feature branches are typically created from the main or develop branch and are used to implement a specific feature, bug fix, or experiment.

bash

git checkout -b feature-login main
In this example:

- git checkout -b feature-login: Creates and switches to the new feature-login branch.

- main: The base branch from which the feature branch is created.

Best Practices for Managing Feature Branches:

- **Create a new branch for each feature**: Always create a new branch for every feature or bug fix. This keeps the work isolated and ensures that other team members can continue working without interference.

  Example:

  bash

  git checkout -b feature-login main

- **Keep feature branches small and focused**: Limit the scope of each feature branch to a single feature or bug fix. This makes it easier to review and merge the changes.
- **Integrate frequently**: Periodically merge or rebase the feature branch with the latest version of the main codebase to stay up-to-date with other changes and avoid conflicts when it's time to merge back.

4. Using Git Flow and Other Branching Strategies

Git Flow is a branching model that introduces a set of guidelines for handling development workflows. It is designed to help developers work with multiple release versions, feature branches, and hotfixes in a systematic and organized way.

Git Flow Overview:

Git Flow involves the following key branches:

- **Main (master)**: The main branch that holds production-ready code.
- **Develop**: The branch where features are integrated before being merged into main.
- **Feature branches**: Used to develop new features or fixes.
- **Release branches**: Created to prepare a new version of the software.
- **Hotfix branches**: Used to quickly patch production releases.

Git Flow Commands:

1. **Start a new feature**:

   bash

   git flow feature start feature-name

2. **Finish a feature**:

bash

git flow feature finish feature-name

3. **Start a release**:

bash

git flow release start version-number

4. **Finish a release**:

bash

git flow release finish version-number

5. **Start a hotfix**:

bash

git flow hotfix start hotfix-name

6. **Finish a hotfix**:

bash

git flow hotfix finish hotfix-name

Other Branching Strategies:

1. **GitHub Flow**: A simplified version of Git Flow, suitable for teams working with continuous deployment. GitHub Flow suggests that developers create feature branches from main, work on them, and submit pull requests for integration.
2. **GitLab Flow**: Combines Git Flow with issue tracking. GitLab Flow introduces environments for continuous delivery.

In this chapter, we covered several advanced Git branching techniques, including **merge vs. rebase**, **managing long-lived branches**, **working with feature branches**, and **using Git Flow and other branching strategies**. Mastering these techniques will help you manage complex workflows, collaborate effectively with your team, and maintain a clean and efficient Git history.

CHAPTER 9: GIT STASH AND OTHER INTERMEDIATE COMMANDS

When working with Git, there are times when you need to put aside your current changes and focus on something else—whether it's switching branches, pulling new updates, or debugging an issue. Git provides several tools to manage these situations without losing your work or cluttering your commit history. Among these tools are **git stash**, **git reset**, **git revert**, and **git diff**.

This chapter dives into these intermediate commands and explains how to use them effectively in your daily development workflow.

1. Using Git Stash to Save Uncommitted Changes

What is git stash?

The **git stash** command allows you to temporarily save (or "stash") changes that you've made in your working directory, without committing them. This is particularly useful when you need to switch branches or pull new updates but don't want to commit incomplete or experimental changes yet. Stashing lets you save your work and return to it later, keeping your working directory clean.

How to Use git stash

Imagine you're working on a new feature in your feature-xyz branch, and you've made some changes, but you suddenly need to switch to the main branch to check something out. Instead of committing unfinished work or discarding it, you can stash it:

bash

git stash

This command will:

- Save the changes you've made to your tracked files (modifications and staged files).
- Revert the files in your working directory back to their last committed state, allowing you to switch to another branch or make other changes.

Viewing Stashed Changes

If you want to see the list of all the stashes you've created, use:

bash

git stash list

This will display a list of all stashes in the format:

bash

stash@{0}: WIP on feature-xyz: abc1234 Added login form

stash@{1}: WIP on feature-xyz: def5678 Added button styles

Each stash is referenced by an index (e.g., stash@{0}). You can use this reference to apply, pop, or drop stashes as needed.

Applying Stashed Changes

To bring back the changes you stashed earlier, you can use:

bash

git stash apply

This command will apply the most recent stash, but it will **not** remove the stash from the list, allowing you to reuse it if necessary.

If you want to apply a specific stash, use the stash reference:

bash

git stash apply stash@{1}

Popping Stashed Changes

If you want to both apply and remove the stash from your stash list, you can use:

bash

git stash pop

This is particularly useful if you've finished working with a particular stash and want to clean up your stash list after applying the changes.

Dropping Stashes

If you no longer need a particular stash and want to delete it, use:

bash

git stash drop stash@{0}

This will remove the specified stash from the list without applying its changes.

The Importance of git stash pop and git stash list

- **git stash pop**: This command is particularly useful when you need to save changes temporarily and return to them later. By applying and removing the stash in one step, it ensures that you're not cluttering your stash list with old, irrelevant stashes.

- **git stash list**: This command helps you keep track of all your stashes. As you work through multiple changes or experiment with different solutions, it's essential to know which stashes are still pending or have been applied.

2. Git Reset and Git Revert: Undoing Changes

What is git reset?

The **git reset** command is used to undo changes in your repository, either by moving the current branch pointer or by removing changes from your working directory and staging area.

Types of Reset:

- **Soft Reset** (git reset --soft): This option moves the HEAD to a previous commit but leaves your working directory and staging area intact. The changes will be available in the staging area for re-committing.

Example:

bash

git reset --soft HEAD~1

This command moves the HEAD back one commit, but the changes from that commit are still staged, so you can amend or re-commit them.

- **Mixed Reset** (git reset --mixed): This is the default behavior of git reset. It moves the HEAD and updates the staging area, but your working directory is unaffected. This is useful if you want to unstage files without losing the changes.

Example:

bash

git reset HEAD~1

This command will unstage the most recent commit but keep the changes in your working directory.

- **Hard Reset** (git reset --hard): This is a more drastic form of reset. It moves the HEAD and updates both the staging area and working directory to reflect the state of a previous commit. This means any uncommitted changes will be lost permanently.

Example:

bash

git reset --hard HEAD~1

This command will remove the last commit and discard any changes in your working directory and staging area.

What is git revert?

Unlike git reset, which rewrites commit history, **git revert** creates a new commit that undoes the changes introduced by a previous commit. This is a safer operation, especially in shared repositories, as it doesn't alter the commit history.

How to Use git revert:

To revert a commit, use the following command:

bash

git revert <commit-id>

This command generates a new commit that effectively reverses the changes made by the commit with <commit-id>. Unlike git reset, the history of commits remains intact, making it ideal for collaborative projects.

Differences Between git reset and git revert

- **git reset** is used when you want to modify the commit history and possibly discard changes from the staging area or working directory.
- **git revert** is used when you want to undo changes but preserve the commit history. It's the safer option in a shared repository, as it doesn't rewrite history.

3. Understanding git diff for Comparing Changes

One of the most common tasks when working with Git is comparing changes: you want to see what has changed in your working directory, between commits, or between branches. This is where **git diff** comes in handy.

What is git diff?

The **git diff** command shows the differences between various Git objects: the working directory, staging area, and previous commits. You can use it to compare files and view changes at different stages in your workflow.

Using git diff

1. **Comparing Working Directory with Staging Area:**

   If you want to see what changes you've made in your working directory that haven't yet been staged, use:

bash

git diff

This will show you the line-by-line differences between the working directory and the staging area.

2. **Comparing Staging Area with Latest Commit:**

To see what changes are staged but not yet committed, use:

bash

git diff --cached

This will compare the staged changes with the last commit.

3. **Comparing Two Commits:**

To compare the differences between two commits, use:

bash

git diff <commit-id1> <commit-id2>

This command will show you the differences between the two specified commits.

4. **Comparing Branches:**

If you want to see the differences between two branches (for example, main and feature-branch), you can run:

bash

git diff main..feature-branch

This will show you the differences between the two branches.

Other Useful git diff Options:

- **git diff --name-only**: Shows only the names of the files that have changed, without displaying the actual changes.
- **git diff --stat**: Displays a summary of changes, showing how many lines have been added or removed in each file.
- **git diff -w**: Ignores whitespace changes when comparing differences.

In this chapter, we've covered several powerful Git commands that can significantly improve your workflow, including **git stash**, **git reset**, **git revert**, and **git diff**. These intermediate commands allow you to save your uncommitted changes temporarily, undo unwanted commits, and compare differences between various states in your project.

Mastering these tools is essential for managing your code effectively, especially in complex projects where collaboration, frequent changes, and careful version control are key to success. By using **git stash**, **git reset**, **git revert**, and **git diff** correctly, you'll be able to maintain a clean, efficient, and organized Git repository, whether you're working solo or as part of a team.

CHAPTER 10: WORKING WITH GIT TAGS

Git tags are a powerful feature that allows you to mark specific points in your repository's history as important. Whether you're marking a release, a milestone, or simply want to create a reference to a particular commit, tags provide an easy way to label and navigate through the history of your project.

In this chapter, we will explore the concept of **Git tags**, how to use them, and best practices for tagging releases.

1. What Are Git Tags and How to Use Them?

Understanding Git Tags

Git tags are references to specific commits in your Git repository, much like branches, but they are **immutable**. Once a tag is created, it doesn't change—it always points to the same commit. Git tags are commonly used to mark version points (e.g., v1.0, v2.0) or important milestones in a project's history, such as a major update or a release candidate.

The key difference between a tag and a branch in Git is that a **branch** is used to keep developing and changing the code, whereas a **tag** is a fixed point that never changes after being created.

There are two types of tags in Git:

1. **Lightweight Tags**: A lightweight tag is essentially just a pointer to a commit. It's like a branch that doesn't change, without any additional metadata.
2. **Annotated Tags**: Annotated tags are more robust. They contain additional information such as the tagger's name,

email, date, and a message, and they are stored as full objects in Git's database.

Why Use Git Tags?

Tags are particularly useful for:

- **Versioning releases**: Tagging commits that represent specific versions of your software, such as v1.0, v2.0, etc.
- **Marking important points**: For example, a tag could mark when a new feature was completed or when a critical bug fix was applied.
- **Sharing and collaboration**: Tags are often used when pushing code to remote repositories (like GitHub) to mark a version for distribution or sharing.

2. Creating Lightweight and Annotated Tags

Creating Lightweight Tags

A lightweight tag is the simplest form of a tag. It is just a name that points to a specific commit in your repository. To create a lightweight tag, use the following command:

bash

git tag <tag-name>

For example, if you want to create a lightweight tag named v1.0 pointing to the latest commit:

bash

git tag v1.0

This command creates a tag at the current HEAD of your repository, meaning it points to the most recent commit. If you want to tag a specific commit (not necessarily the most recent one), you can provide the commit hash as an argument:

bash

git tag v1.0 <commit-hash>

Creating Annotated Tags

Annotated tags are more informative. They include the tagger's name, email, and a timestamp, and they can also contain a message. To create an annotated tag, use the -a option along with the -m flag to add a message:

bash

git tag -a <tag-name> -m "Tagging version 1.0 release"

For example, to create an annotated tag for the v1.0 release:

bash

git tag -a v1.0 -m "Version 1.0 release"

Annotated tags are stored as full objects in Git, meaning they are more persistent and provide additional metadata compared to lightweight tags. This is the preferred tag type when you want to provide a meaningful description of the tagged version.

Tagging a Specific Commit

You can also create a tag for a commit that's not the most recent by providing the commit hash:

bash

git tag -a v1.0 <commit-hash> -m "Tagging version 1.0 release"
This allows you to tag a version of the project at a specific point in time, even if that commit is older than your current HEAD.

3. Pushing Tags to a Remote Repository

Once you've created tags locally, you might want to push them to a remote repository like GitHub to share them with collaborators or make them available for distribution. By default, Git does not push tags to the remote repository automatically when you perform a git push.

To push a specific tag to a remote repository, use:

bash

git push origin <tag-name>

For example, to push the v1.0 tag:

bash

git push origin v1.0

If you want to push **all tags** at once, use the following command:

bash

git push --tags

This command pushes all tags that exist in your local repository to the remote repository.

Checking Pushed Tags

Once you've pushed a tag to a remote repository, you can verify that it has been successfully uploaded by running:

bash

git ls-remote --tags origin

This command lists all the tags that have been pushed to the remote repository.

4. Best Practices for Tagging Releases

Git tags are essential for versioning your software and marking important milestones. Here are some best practices for working with tags, especially when it comes to tagging releases:

1. Use Semantic Versioning

One of the most widely adopted practices for versioning software is **Semantic Versioning** (SemVer). According to SemVer, version numbers are broken down into three parts: **MAJOR.MINOR.PATCH**.

- **MAJOR** version is incremented when there are incompatible API changes.
- **MINOR** version is incremented when new features are added in a backward-compatible manner.
- **PATCH** version is incremented when backward-compatible bug fixes are made.

For example:

- v1.0.0 – Initial release
- v1.1.0 – New feature added (backward-compatible)
- v2.0.0 – Major change with breaking API changes

By following SemVer, you can clearly communicate what changes have been made between releases, and your users can better understand how new versions affect their usage of the software.

2. Tag Releases with Clear, Descriptive Messages

When creating tags, always include clear, meaningful commit messages. For annotated tags, this is easy, as Git allows you to specify a tag message. For lightweight tags, ensure that the tag name itself clearly conveys what the tag represents (e.g., v1.2.0, hotfix-2023-07-01, etc.).

3. Tag Releases, Not Every Commit

It's important not to tag every single commit. Instead, tag only **major releases**, **milestones**, or **important checkpoints** in your project. This helps to avoid cluttering your repository with unnecessary tags and makes it easier to navigate your project history.

4. Ensure Tags Are Part of the Release Process

Make tagging a part of your release process. Whether you're releasing a version of the software internally or externally, tagging the release ensures that you can easily access the exact commit associated with that release. It's a great way to keep your release history organized and track changes over time.

5. Use Tags for Stable Versions

Tags are ideal for marking **stable versions** of your software. When you're ready to release a version of your software (e.g., v1.0), create a tag. This allows your team and your users to easily refer to that exact version. If any bugs are discovered after the release, you can quickly reference the exact commit by its tag.

6. Use Tags for Distribution

If you're distributing software (e.g., through a package manager or deployment system), tags provide an easy way to refer to the version of the software you're distributing. By tagging your release and pushing it to a remote repository, you ensure that the release version is easily accessible to others.

7. Avoid Overwriting Tags

Once you push a tag to a remote repository, it is generally best practice **not to overwrite it**. If you need to change a tag, you can delete the old one and create a new tag, but avoid modifying tags that have already been shared with others.

If you do need to delete a tag, use:

bash

git tag -d <tag-name>

To remove the tag from the remote repository:

bash

git push --delete origin <tag-name>

In this chapter, we have covered the fundamentals of working with Git tags, including how to create and manage them, push tags to remote repositories, and adopt best practices for versioning releases. Tags are an essential part of any developer's toolkit, especially when managing releases and important milestones in your project.

By following the best practices outlined in this chapter, you can ensure that your tags are meaningful, easy to use, and beneficial for both your team and any external collaborators or users. Whether you're marking the start of a major version or simply keeping track of key project points, Git tags help you maintain a well-organized and accessible project history.

CHAPTER 11: GIT CONFIGURATION AND OPTIMIZATION

Git is a powerful tool, but for developers to fully harness its capabilities, it's essential to configure it properly and optimize its performance, especially when working with large projects. Proper Git configuration ensures that your workflows are more efficient, your collaboration with team members runs smoothly, and your Git operations, like cloning, fetching, and pushing, are as fast as possible.

This chapter delves into configuring Git for individual and team use, optimizing performance, and creating shortcuts for common tasks. Whether you're working on personal projects or collaborating with large teams, optimizing your Git setup can significantly streamline your workflow.

1. Configuring Global and Local Settings

Global Configuration vs. Local Configuration

Git allows you to set configuration options at three different levels:

- **System-wide**: These configurations apply to all users and repositories on your system. They are typically set by system administrators.

- **Global**: These configurations apply to all Git repositories for a particular user. For example, you can configure your username, email, and other preferences so that you don't have to repeat the setup for each project.

- **Local**: These configurations apply only to a specific Git repository. For example, you might want to configure a different username or email for a particular project.

By default, Git looks at local settings first, then global settings, and finally system-wide settings.

Setting Global Configuration

To set your global Git configuration, use the following commands. This will configure your username, email, and preferred text editor.

bash

git config --global user.name "Your Name"
git config --global user.email "your.email@example.com"
git config --global core.editor "vim"

The --global flag tells Git to apply these settings to all of your repositories. This is useful for setting your identity (name and email) and preferred editor. However, you can override these settings for specific repositories (see the section on local settings).

Setting Local Configuration

Sometimes you might want to use different configuration settings for a specific repository (e.g., a different email address for a work project). To set local configurations, run the same git config command without the --global flag while inside the project directory:

bash

git config user.name "Work Name"
git config user.email "work.email@example.com"
This applies only to the repository you are currently working on, not globally.

View Your Git Configuration
To see the current configuration settings (global and local) for Git, use the command:

bash

git config --list
This will list all of your Git configuration values, including global and local settings. If you want to see only global settings, you can use:

bash

git config --global --list

If you are troubleshooting or just want to see all of the configuration values Git is using for a specific repository, you can check the local configuration file by opening .git/config in the project directory.

2. Git Aliases for Faster Workflows

Git aliases are shortcuts for frequently used Git commands, helping to speed up your workflow by reducing the number of keystrokes and simplifying complex commands. Instead of typing out long, repetitive commands, you can create custom aliases that are easier to remember and faster to execute.

Creating Git Aliases

To create a Git alias, you can use the git config command. Here are a few useful examples of custom aliases:

- **Shortening git status**: If you find yourself typing git status often, you can create an alias for it like this:

  bash

  git config --global alias.st status
  Now, instead of typing git status, you can type git st.

- **Alias for git log with pretty formatting**: Instead of typing git log --oneline --graph --decorate, you can create an alias:

bash

git config --global alias.lg "log --oneline --graph --decorate"

Now, you can simply type git lg for a more visually informative log output.

- **Alias for checking out branches**: If you often switch branches, you can create a simple alias:

bash

git config --global alias.co checkout

Afterward, you can use git co <branch-name> instead of git checkout <branch-name>.

Viewing and Managing Aliases

To see a list of all your aliases, you can open the global Git configuration file (~/.gitconfig) or use:

bash

git config --global --list

You can also edit the .gitconfig file manually if you prefer to manage aliases directly. Just open the file in your preferred text editor and modify or add new aliases under the [alias] section.

More Complex Aliases

You can also create more complex aliases involving multiple commands. For example, if you frequently perform a pull and rebase, you can create a custom alias for that:

bash

```
git config --global alias.prb "!git pull --rebase"
```

Now, you can simply run git prb to pull and rebase in one command.

3. Configuring Git for Team Collaboration

When collaborating on a project with a team, there are several Git configuration options that can help streamline workflows and ensure that your team is using Git efficiently.

Configuring User Identity for Team Projects

In a collaborative environment, it's important that every contributor uses the correct username and email address, especially if they are contributing from multiple devices. To ensure that Git tracks the correct identity for each contributor, configure both global and local user information.

For team projects, it's common practice to set local configuration values for each repository, especially if you are contributing to open-source projects or projects with multiple team members:

bash

git config user.name "Team Member Name"
git config user.email "teammember.email@example.com"
This ensures that Git logs the correct identity for each contributor and helps keep the project history clear and accurate.

Enforcing Consistent Commit Messages

One of the easiest ways to ensure collaboration runs smoothly is to standardize your commit messages. You can configure Git to require a specific format for commit messages, such as a prefix like feat, fix, or chore for each commit type. For example, you can create a .gitmessage template to enforce consistency.

Create a file called .gitmessage in your repository or home directory and add your desired format:

bash

git config --global commit.template ~/.gitmessage

This ensures that each commit message starts with a defined structure, reducing errors and keeping your commit history organized.

Setting Up Remotes for Team Collaboration

When working with a team, you'll often be pushing and pulling changes to and from remote repositories (such as GitHub, GitLab, or Bitbucket). You can add remote repositories using:

bash

git remote add origin https://github.com/username/repo.git

This allows Git to know where to push and pull changes from. You can also set up multiple remotes (e.g., one for development and one for staging) and specify which one you want to interact with using git push or git pull:

bash

git remote add staging https://github.com/username/staging-repo.git

To push to a specific remote:

bash

git push staging main

Configuring SSH for Remote Authentication

For easier and more secure access to remote repositories, you should configure SSH keys to authenticate your Git sessions, rather than using your username and password every time. To set up SSH:

1. Generate an SSH key pair (if you don't have one):

    bash

    ssh-keygen -t rsa -b 4096 -C "your.email@example.com"

2. Add your SSH key to the SSH agent:

    bash

    eval "$(ssh-agent -s)"
    ssh-add ~/.ssh/id_rsa

3. Add the public key (~/.ssh/id_rsa.pub) to your Git hosting service (e.g., GitHub, GitLab, Bitbucket).

Now you can clone, push, and pull from your repositories without needing to enter your username and password each time.

4. Performance Optimization for Large Repositories

Git is incredibly fast, but as repositories grow in size (especially with large files, many commits, or many branches), performance can degrade. Fortunately, there are several strategies to optimize Git for working with large repositories.

Shallow Clones

If you only need the latest version of a repository (and not the full history), you can create a **shallow clone**. A shallow clone only contains the latest commit history, significantly reducing the size of the repository:

bash

git clone --depth 1 https://github.com/username/repo.git

This command clones only the latest commit (depth 1) instead of the entire history. It's especially useful when you don't need to access the full history of a repository.

Using Git LFS (Large File Storage)

Git LFS is an extension for handling large files such as images, videos, and datasets. By using Git LFS, large files are stored outside of the Git repository while still being versioned and tracked by Git.

To install Git LFS, run:

bash

git lfs install

You can then track specific file types with:

bash

git lfs track "*.jpg"

This will ensure that large files are managed efficiently, keeping the repository size manageable while still enabling version control.

Garbage Collection

Over time, Git repositories can accumulate unnecessary files and objects that may slow down performance. To clean up and optimize your repository, run Git's **garbage collection**:

bash

git gc --aggressive

This command removes unreachable objects and optimizes your repository for better performance.

Configuring and optimizing Git is crucial for both individual and team workflows. By setting global and local configurations, creating aliases for repetitive tasks, and optimizing performance for large repositories, you can significantly improve your development experience and make Git a more powerful tool in your arsenal. Whether you're working alone or as part of a team, these strategies will help you get the most out of Git's features.

CHAPTER 12: UNDERSTANDING GIT WORKFLOWS

Git workflows are essential for managing how code is developed, integrated, and released in a collaborative environment. When teams work together, it's important to have a set of rules and strategies to maintain smooth and effective collaboration. These workflows ensure that developers can work on different tasks and features concurrently without stepping on each other's toes, while also allowing for efficient integration and deployment of code.

This chapter introduces common Git workflows used by teams and organizations, outlines the most popular workflows, and discusses how to choose the right one for your project. It also covers how Git integrates with Continuous Integration (CI) and Continuous

Deployment (CD) systems to automate testing and deployment processes.

1. Git Workflows for Teams and Organizations

What is a Git Workflow?

A Git workflow is a set of conventions or practices that define how different team members interact with a Git repository. It lays out how branches should be created, how features are integrated, how releases are handled, and how code is shared among team members. A well-defined workflow makes collaboration easier and more efficient while minimizing the risk of conflicts and errors.

For teams and organizations, choosing the right workflow is crucial for maintaining productivity, code quality, and ensuring smooth collaboration. Without a defined workflow, developers may find themselves in situations where they overwrite each other's work, create redundant code, or face difficulties during code review and integration.

There are various workflows used by different types of teams. The choice of workflow depends on the size of the team, the complexity of the project, and the deployment requirements.

Key Aspects of Git Workflows:

- **Branching strategy**: How branches are created and managed.

- **Release management**: How features are integrated into the main product.

- **Collaboration flow**: How developers push, pull, and share their code.

- **Integration practices**: How code is reviewed and merged.

- **Deployment practices**: How and when code is released.

2. Popular Git Workflows

There are several widely-used Git workflows that have proven effective in different types of development environments. Below, we'll cover the three most popular workflows: Git Flow, GitHub Flow, and GitLab Flow.

Git Flow

Git Flow is a branching model that was introduced by Vincent Driessen. It's a well-structured workflow primarily used in larger teams or projects with scheduled releases and complex deployment processes. Git Flow splits the development process into specific, well-defined branches, making it ideal for handling large releases with multiple feature sets and stages.

Key branches in Git Flow:

- **master**: Contains the stable production-ready code.
- **develop**: The main integration branch for features and fixes.
- **feature branches**: Created from develop for developing new features.
- **release branches**: Created from develop when preparing for a new release.
- **hotfix branches**: Created from master to fix urgent bugs in production.

Workflow Process:

1. **Feature Development**: New features are developed in individual feature branches, which are based on the develop branch.
2. **Release Preparation**: When the features are ready, a release branch is created from develop. This branch is for preparing the code for release, including final bug fixes, version bumps, and other final preparations.
3. **Release Merge**: Once the release is ready, it is merged into both master and develop to ensure that both branches have the latest stable code.
4. **Hotfix**: If critical bugs are found in the production (in the master branch), a hotfix branch is created. The hotfix is then merged into both master and develop.

When to use Git Flow:

- Ideal for large teams and projects where stable releases and careful management of features are required.
- Projects with defined release cycles (e.g., every month or quarter).
- Suitable for projects that need to support multiple versions of the software simultaneously.

Downsides of Git Flow:

- Can be complex and slow for small teams or quick development cycles.
- Requires a lot of branching and merging, which may lead to additional overhead.

GitHub Flow

GitHub Flow is a simpler, more streamlined workflow that is popular with smaller teams and agile development processes. GitHub Flow encourages rapid development, continuous integration, and immediate deployment, making it ideal for teams that need to move fast and release often.

Key branches in GitHub Flow:

- **main** (or master): The main production branch that always contains the stable code.

- **feature branches**: Used for all new features, bug fixes, or improvements. Each new feature is developed in its own branch, which is created from main.

Workflow Process:

1. **Create a Feature Branch**: Developers create a new branch for every task (feature or bug fix) they are working on.
2. **Make Changes**: All changes are made to the feature branch. Once development is complete, the branch is pushed to the remote repository on GitHub.
3. **Create a Pull Request (PR)**: A pull request is created to propose merging the feature branch back into the main branch. The PR serves as a discussion and review space where team members can comment on the changes.
4. **Code Review and Merge**: Once the pull request is reviewed and approved, it is merged into the main branch. The main branch always contains deployable, production-ready code.
5. **Deploy**: After the merge, the code is deployed directly to production (via CI/CD pipelines).

When to use GitHub Flow:

- Ideal for teams working on continuous delivery or integration with fast release cycles.

- Suitable for smaller teams and startups that need to release quickly and frequently.
- Works well for teams using GitHub as their primary platform for collaboration.

Downsides of GitHub Flow:

- Lack of dedicated staging or pre-release branches could make testing and stabilization harder for large or complex releases.
- Less suited for teams working on large, multi-version projects that need rigid release cycles.

GitLab Flow

GitLab Flow combines the best elements of both Git Flow and GitHub Flow. It is an adaptable workflow that is designed to cater to both feature-driven development and continuous delivery models. GitLab Flow can accommodate more complex workflows by allowing teams to create environments (such as production, staging, or development) as part of the branching model.

Key branches in GitLab Flow:

- **master**: The production-ready branch.
- **feature branches**: For developing new features.
- **environment branches**: For staging or testing code before deployment.

- **release branches**: For managing code that's ready for deployment.

Workflow Process:

1. **Feature Development**: Developers create feature branches from master or development depending on the complexity of the task.
2. **Create Merge Request (MR)**: After completing the feature, a merge request is created for the feature branch to be merged into the master branch.
3. **Staging and Testing**: The code goes through staging or QA environments, where it is tested before being deployed to production.
4. **Production Deployment**: Once the code passes the tests and is ready for production, it is merged into master and deployed.

When to use GitLab Flow:

- Suitable for teams that need to integrate staging environments with their Git workflow.
- Great for teams that need a flexible and scalable workflow with more complex deployment pipelines.
- Ideal for teams using GitLab for their repository management, CI/CD, and issue tracking.

Downsides of GitLab Flow:

- May be overkill for small teams or projects that do not require complex environments or deployment pipelines.

3. Choosing the Right Workflow for Your Project

When choosing a Git workflow for your team or organization, consider the following factors:

- **Team Size**: Small teams may benefit from simpler workflows like GitHub Flow, while larger teams with complex release cycles may need the structure of Git Flow or GitLab Flow.
- **Project Complexity**: If your project requires handling multiple versions or large feature sets, Git Flow may be more appropriate. For rapid iteration and continuous deployment, GitHub Flow or GitLab Flow may be a better fit.
- **Deployment Frequency**: Teams with frequent releases or those practicing continuous integration and delivery (CI/CD) may lean towards GitHub Flow or GitLab Flow.
- **Branching Needs**: If you need to support multiple environments (e.g., development, staging, production), GitLab Flow's support for environment branches may be ideal.

Ultimately, the choice of workflow should reflect the needs of your team, the size and complexity of the project, and the desired speed of development and release.

4. Integrating with Continuous Integration/Continuous Deployment (CI/CD)

CI/CD is a set of practices that automate the integration, testing, and deployment of code. Git workflows can be enhanced by integrating them with CI/CD pipelines to improve efficiency and speed. CI/CD allows teams to automate tasks like building, testing, and deploying code, ensuring that code changes are properly validated and deployed as soon as they are merged into the main branch.

Continuous Integration (CI)

CI refers to the practice of automatically integrating new code changes into a shared repository several times a day. Every time a developer pushes changes to the repository, the CI system runs automated tests to validate the code. If tests pass, the code is integrated into the main branch; if tests fail, the CI system alerts the team.

Continuous Deployment (CD)

CD extends the concept of CI by automatically deploying the validated code to production. Every time code is merged into the main branch, the CD pipeline ensures that it is deployed to production with minimal human intervention.

How CI/CD Integrates with Git Workflows

Most Git workflows, such as GitHub Flow and GitLab Flow, integrate seamlessly with CI/CD tools. When a developer creates a pull request or merge request, the CI/CD system automatically runs tests, performs builds, and ensures that the code is production-ready before merging it into the main branch.

By integrating CI/CD, teams can ensure that only stable, tested code makes it to production, reducing the risk of introducing bugs and improving the overall quality of the product.

Git workflows are critical for managing collaborative software development, ensuring that developers can work together efficiently and effectively. By selecting the right Git workflow for your team's needs and integrating it with CI/CD pipelines, you can streamline development, reduce errors, and improve the quality of your product. Whether you choose Git Flow, GitHub Flow, or GitLab Flow, each workflow provides a structure that can be adapted to fit the unique needs of your project.

CHAPTER 13: GIT HOOKS: AUTOMATING PROCESSES

Git hooks are scripts that Git executes before or after certain Git commands, allowing you to automate processes, enforce rules, and integrate additional tools into your development workflow. They provide a powerful way to streamline and enhance your Git operations, ensuring that tasks like code quality checks, testing, and deployments are consistently handled without manual intervention.

This chapter explores the concept of Git hooks in detail, how they work, and how to use them effectively. We will cover the most commonly used hooks, such as pre-commit, post-merge, and post-checkout, as well as integrating them with automated testing tools to improve the overall quality and efficiency of your development pipeline.

1. What Are Git Hooks?

Git hooks are scripts that are triggered by specific Git commands, allowing you to run custom actions at different points in the Git workflow. Hooks can be written in various scripting languages such as Bash, Python, or Ruby, and they reside in the .git/hooks directory of your Git repository.

There are two categories of hooks:

- **Client-side hooks**: These run on the local machine, typically when interacting with the repository directly. Examples include pre-commit, post-checkout, and pre-push.
- **Server-side hooks**: These are triggered on the server, usually to perform checks or actions when pushing or pulling code to and from a remote repository. Examples include pre-receive, update, and post-receive.

Each hook is executed when a specific Git operation is performed. For example, a pre-commit hook runs before a commit is finalized, and a post-merge hook runs after a merge is completed.

Example of a Hook File

In the .git/hooks directory, you'll find sample hook scripts that have .sample extensions. For example, pre-commit.sample is the sample pre-commit hook. You can rename it by removing the .sample extension and modify it according to your needs. Each hook script can contain commands or scripts that you want to execute at that point in the Git workflow.

2. Using Pre-Commit Hooks for Code Quality

The **pre-commit** hook is one of the most commonly used Git hooks. It runs automatically before a commit is finalized and is ideal for enforcing code quality rules and performing checks. This hook provides an excellent opportunity to prevent common mistakes like committing code with syntax errors, failing tests, or other issues that could affect the quality of the codebase.

Typical Use Cases for pre-commit Hooks:

- **Linting**: Run a linter to check code style violations.
- **Syntax Checking**: Ensure that code has no syntax errors before committing.

- **Automated Testing**: Run unit tests or integration tests to ensure that the new code doesn't break existing functionality.

Example: Linting with pre-commit

You can set up a pre-commit hook to run a JavaScript linter, such as ESLint, before every commit to ensure code adheres to style guidelines. Here's an example of what the script might look like in .git/hooks/pre-commit:

bash

```
#!/bin/sh


# Run ESLint on all staged JavaScript files
eslint $(git diff --cached --name-only --diff-filter=ACM | grep '\.js$')


# If ESLint fails, exit with a non-zero code, preventing the commit
if [ $? -ne 0 ]; then
    echo "Linting failed. Commit aborted."
    exit 1
fi
```

This script checks for .js files that are staged for commit, runs ESLint on them, and prevents the commit if there are any linting errors.

Integrating Pre-Commit with Tools like prettier or eslint

A popular setup involves using the pre-commit framework, which allows you to easily integrate multiple hooks for tasks like code formatting, linting, and testing. Here's an example of integrating prettier (a code formatter) and eslint into your pre-commit hook using the pre-commit framework:

1. **Install the pre-commit tool**:

bash

pip install pre-commit

2. **Create a .pre-commit-config.yaml file** in your repository root:

yaml

- repo: https://github.com/prettier/prettier
  rev: v2.3.0
  hooks:
  - id: prettier
    files: \.(js|ts|css|json|md)$

- repo: https://github.com/eslint/eslint
  rev: v7.32.0
  hooks:

```
-  id: eslint
   files: \.js$
```

3. **Install the hooks**:

```
bash


pre-commit install
```

Now, every time a developer commits, the pre-commit framework will automatically run prettier and eslint to ensure that code is well-formatted and error-free.

3. Setting Up Post-Merge and Post-Checkout Hooks

In addition to the pre-commit hook, there are several other hooks that can automate tasks following specific Git operations. Two useful hooks are the post-merge and post-checkout hooks.

Post-Merge Hook

The **post-merge** hook is executed after a merge operation is completed. This hook is commonly used to trigger actions that should occur after changes are merged into the current branch. For example, you might want to trigger a build, run tests, or synchronize dependencies after merging.

Example: Running Tests After a Merge

Suppose your project includes integration tests that should be run every time a merge is completed. You could set up a post-merge hook like the following:

bash

```
#!/bin/sh

# Run tests after merge
echo "Running tests after merge..."
npm test

if [ $? -ne 0 ]; then
    echo "Tests failed. Please resolve the issues."
    exit 1
fi
```

This script runs the tests in your Node.js project, ensuring that the merge did not introduce any regressions.

Post-Checkout Hook

The **post-checkout** hook is triggered after a git checkout operation is completed. It's often used to automate tasks that should occur after switching branches, such as setting up the environment or synchronizing local files.

Example: Installing Dependencies After Checkout

If your project requires specific dependencies when switching branches, you can use the post-checkout hook to automatically install them:

bash

```
#!/bin/sh
```

```
# Install dependencies when switching branches
if [ -f package.json ]; then
    echo "Installing dependencies..."
    npm install
fi
```

This ensures that your local environment is always up-to-date with the required dependencies for the branch you're working on.

4. Integrating Git Hooks with Automated Testing Tools

One of the most powerful uses of Git hooks is to integrate them with automated testing tools to ensure code quality before it's committed, merged, or deployed. Automated testing tools can be configured to run tests whenever a Git hook is triggered, helping to catch bugs and regressions early in the development process.

Common Automated Testing Tools Integrated with Git Hooks:

- **JUnit**: For running unit tests in Java projects.

- **Mocha/Chai**: For testing JavaScript/Node.js applications.
- **PyTest**: For running tests in Python projects.
- **Selenium**: For end-to-end testing in web applications.

Example: Automating Tests with Git Hooks

For instance, let's integrate a Python testing tool, **PyTest**, into a pre-commit hook to run unit tests before committing changes:

bash

```
#!/bin/sh

# Run PyTest before committing
echo "Running PyTest tests..."
pytest tests/

if [ $? -ne 0 ]; then
    echo "Tests failed. Commit aborted."
    exit 1
fi
```

This ensures that no code is committed unless all tests pass, improving the reliability of your codebase.

Git hooks provide a powerful mechanism for automating processes and enforcing best practices in your development workflow. By setting up hooks like pre-commit, post-merge, and post-checkout, you can automate tasks such as code linting, running tests, and synchronizing dependencies. Integrating Git hooks with automated testing tools ensures that code quality remains high, reducing the risk of bugs and errors in production.

Whether you're enforcing coding standards, automating testing, or managing deployments, Git hooks are a valuable tool for streamlining development workflows and ensuring consistency across teams.

CHAPTER 14: DEBUGGING WITH GIT

Debugging is a critical part of software development, and having the right tools at your disposal can significantly reduce the time spent identifying and fixing issues. Git, as a powerful version control system, offers several features that can help you efficiently debug your code, track down regressions, and fix mistakes in your commit history. This chapter explores some of the best Git features for debugging, including git bisect, git reset, git checkout, and git reflog.

1. Using git bisect to Find the Commit that Introduced a Bug

When you're working with a codebase and a bug appears, it's often difficult to pinpoint exactly when the bug was introduced, especially if the project has been evolving for a long time. Git's bisect command helps you quickly narrow down the commit that introduced the issue by performing a binary search through the commit history.

What is git bisect?

git bisect works by dividing the commit history into smaller chunks. It requires you to mark a commit as "bad" (where the bug exists) and another as "good" (where the bug does not exist). Git will then check out a commit halfway between the "good" and "bad" commits and ask if the bug is present in that commit. Based on your answer, Git will further divide the history until it finds the exact commit that introduced the issue.

Using git bisect in Practice

1. **Start a bisect session**: First, you need to let Git know you're starting a bisect session. You'll provide two commits: one where the code was working correctly (good) and one where the bug is present (bad).

bash

```
git bisect start
git bisect bad            # Mark the current commit as bad
git bisect good <commit-hash>  # Mark an earlier commit
where the bug wasn't present as good
```

2. **Test intermediate commits**: Git will automatically checkout an intermediate commit between the good and bad commits. You test this commit by running your application or performing the necessary checks to verify if the bug is present.

3. **Mark each commit**:
   - If the bug is present in the tested commit, mark it as "bad":

   bash

   ```
   git bisect bad
   ```

   - If the bug is not present, mark it as "good":

bash

git bisect good

4. **Continue the bisect process**: Git will keep narrowing down the range of commits until it identifies the problematic commit. When it finds the commit that introduced the bug, it will output the commit hash and message.

5. **End the bisect session**: Once you have identified the commit, you can end the bisect session using the following command:

bash

git bisect reset

This will return you to the original state of the branch you were working on.

Example:

Imagine you're working on a project, and after a recent update, a bug appeared. You know the bug didn't exist two weeks ago, but you don't know when it was introduced. Here's how you could use git bisect:

bash

```
git bisect start
git bisect bad            # Mark the current commit as bad
git bisect good <commit-hash>     # Mark the commit from two
weeks ago as good
# Git will check out a commit halfway between the two. Run your
tests to verify.
# Continue marking commits as bad or good based on your testing.
git bisect reset            # Once the problematic commit is found,
reset the bisect session.
```

2. Managing Broken Commits and Reverting Them

Sometimes, when a commit introduces a bug, you may not want to go through the process of debugging it. Instead, you may decide to revert the commit completely to restore the application to its previous working state.

Git provides a few powerful commands to manage broken commits and revert changes effectively:

Reverting a Commit

If you identify a specific commit that is causing issues, you can revert it using git revert. This command creates a new commit that undoes the changes introduced by a previous commit, without altering the project history.

bash

git revert <commit-hash>

This will open your default editor with a commit message like "Revert commit [commit-hash]". You can modify the message if needed, and once you save and close the editor, the revert will be completed.

Reverting Multiple Commits

To revert a range of commits, you can use:

bash

git revert <oldest-commit-hash>^..<newest-commit-hash>

This reverts all commits between the two specified commit hashes. Note that git revert will create a separate commit for each reverted commit.

Reverting the Last Commit

If you need to revert the most recent commit, you can use:

bash

git revert HEAD

This is particularly useful when you realize immediately after committing that a change should not have been made.

Managing Broken Commits with git reset

Sometimes, simply reverting a commit is not enough, especially if the commit is deeply embedded in your development history. In such cases, you might need to reset your repository to a previous state. Git provides the git reset command, which has different modes of operation:

- **Soft reset** (--soft): This resets the commit history to a specific commit but leaves your changes in the working directory and staging area.

  bash

  git reset --soft <commit-hash>

- **Mixed reset** (default): This resets the commit history and staging area, but leaves your working directory unchanged.

  bash

  git reset <commit-hash>

- **Hard reset** (--hard): This resets the commit history, staging area, and working directory. All uncommitted changes will be lost.

  bash

git reset --hard <commit-hash>

Warning: The git reset --hard command can result in the permanent loss of changes. Be cautious when using it.

3. Fixing Mistakes with git reset and git checkout

Sometimes, after making changes, you may realize that you made a mistake—whether it's a commit that should not have been made, or changes that should not have been added to a commit. Git offers several ways to fix such mistakes:

Undoing Local Changes with git reset

If you've made changes that are not yet committed and you want to discard them, you can use git reset to unstage those changes:

bash

git reset <file-path>

This will unstage the file but leave the changes in your working directory. If you want to completely discard the changes (and lose them forever), you can use:

bash

git checkout -- <file-path>

This will revert the file to the version in the latest commit, effectively discarding all local changes.

Undoing Commits with git reset

If you have already committed changes but need to undo them, git reset can help. As mentioned earlier, a soft reset allows you to move the HEAD back to a previous commit while keeping the changes staged:

bash

git reset --soft <commit-hash>

If you just want to reset the history without changing the working directory, use the mixed option:

bash

git reset --mixed <commit-hash>

4. Using git reflog to Recover Lost Commits

Git is a powerful tool for tracking your commit history, but sometimes commits can seem "lost," especially after performing commands like git reset. The git reflog command provides a safety net in these situations by tracking the movement of HEAD and branch pointers.

What is git reflog?

git reflog keeps a log of all the changes to your repository's HEAD, even those that are no longer part of the commit history (like commits that were deleted after a reset). This means that even if you've reset your branch or performed a git checkout to a previous commit, git reflog allows you to recover lost commits.

Using git reflog to Recover Lost Commits

To view the reflog, simply run:

bash

git reflog

This will display a list of all recent changes to the repository, including commits, resets, and checkouts. Each entry is associated with a commit hash.

Once you identify the commit you want to recover, you can simply checkout or reset to that commit:

bash

git checkout <commit-hash>

or

bash

git reset --hard <commit-hash>

This allows you to recover commits that may have been mistakenly lost.

Debugging with Git is an essential skill for every developer. Tools like git bisect, git reset, git checkout, and git reflog can help you efficiently trace the source of bugs, fix mistakes, and recover lost commits. By mastering these Git commands, you'll not only improve your debugging skills but also enhance your overall workflow, ensuring that you can quickly recover from mistakes and continue developing with confidence.

Whether you're working on a solo project or part of a large team, using Git's debugging features effectively can save you time and prevent bugs from slipping through unnoticed.

CHAPTER 15: ADVANCED MERGING TECHNIQUES

Merging is one of the most fundamental and powerful features of Git, enabling developers to integrate changes from different branches seamlessly. However, as with any powerful tool, it comes with its complexities. In this chapter, we'll explore some advanced merging techniques in Git, including handling merge conflicts, resolving them efficiently, and using Git's built-in tools to streamline the process.

1. Understanding Merge Conflicts

Merge conflicts occur when Git is unable to automatically reconcile differences between two branches during a merge operation. This typically happens when two different branches modify the same lines of the same file(s) in incompatible ways. Git will not be able to decide which change to keep, resulting in a conflict that needs to be manually resolved.

Common Scenarios for Merge Conflicts

- **Simultaneous edits on the same line**: When two branches modify the same line of code differently.
- **File additions**: When a file is added to one branch but deleted in another.
- **Renaming and modifying a file**: If a file is renamed in one branch but modified in another, Git will have trouble reconciling these changes.

- **Binary files**: Merge conflicts can also occur with binary files, as Git cannot automatically merge them.

Git's Conflict Markers

When Git encounters a conflict, it will attempt to merge the changes and place special conflict markers in the file to highlight the areas of conflict. The file will contain sections marked like this:

plaintext

```
<<<<<<< HEAD
// Changes from the current branch
=======
 // Changes from the branch you're merging
>>>>>>> feature-branch
```

- **HEAD**: The current branch (the one you're merging into).
- **feature-branch**: The branch you're trying to merge.

It's your job to manually edit the file, choosing between the conflicting changes, or possibly combining them.

2. Advanced Conflict Resolution Strategies

When dealing with merge conflicts, it's important not just to fix them, but to do so in a way that maintains the integrity and functionality of your codebase. Here are some advanced strategies to consider when resolving conflicts:

a. Manual Conflict Resolution

Manual conflict resolution is the most straightforward approach, where you open the file containing the conflict and decide which change to keep or how to combine both sets of changes.

- Open the file and look for the conflict markers (<<<<<<<, =======, >>>>>>>).
- Inspect the changes and understand the context of both sets of changes.
- Decide on the desired final version of the code. This might mean keeping changes from both sides, discarding one side, or combining changes from both.
- After editing, remove the conflict markers and save the file.
- Test the code to ensure it works as expected.

b. Choosing Between Branches Using git checkout

Sometimes, you may want to favor the changes from one branch over the other. Git allows you to check out the version of a file from either the current branch or the branch you're merging.

To keep the changes from the current branch:

bash

git checkout --ours <file-path>

To keep the changes from the branch being merged:

bash

git checkout --theirs <file-path>

This allows you to resolve conflicts quickly without manually editing the conflicting files.

c. Interactive Conflict Resolution

If you want to have more control over how conflicts are resolved, you can use an interactive rebase or cherry-pick operation to split a merge into smaller, more manageable steps. This can help avoid large and complicated conflicts and allows for more granular conflict resolution.

d. Aborting a Merge

If you find that the merge is too complicated or the conflict resolution process is causing more harm than good, you can always abort the merge operation to return to the state before the merge started:

bash

git merge --abort

This will restore your working directory to the state it was in before the merge, and you can attempt the merge again later or use a different strategy.

3. Using Git's Three-Way Merge

Git uses a **three-way merge** when merging changes from two different branches. A three-way merge involves three snapshots of the codebase:

1. **The common ancestor**: The commit where both branches diverged.
2. **The current branch (HEAD)**: The branch you're merging into.
3. **The branch you're merging**: The branch you're merging from.

Git will try to merge the changes from both branches by comparing the changes in these three snapshots. If there are no conflicts between the changes made in the current branch and the branch being merged, Git will automatically complete the merge. However, if both branches have modified the same lines of the same file, Git will be unable to determine the correct version and will create a conflict.

Example of Three-Way Merge

Let's say the common ancestor (commit A) has the following code:

python

```
# A
def add_numbers(a, b):
    return a + b
```

Branch B makes a change to the function:

python

```
# B
def add_numbers(a, b):
    return a + b + 10
```

Branch C also modifies the function, but in a different way:

python

```
# C
def add_numbers(a, b):
    return a + b * 2
```

When Git attempts to merge B and C, it will use the common ancestor A to determine what changed. It will then attempt a three-way merge:

- The changes in B are +10 to the return value.
- The changes in C are multiplying b by 2.

If Git cannot automatically decide how to reconcile these two, it will mark the conflict and ask for manual intervention.

4. Leveraging git mergetool for Visual Merging

For many developers, visual conflict resolution is far easier than resolving conflicts manually using text editors. Git provides the git mergetool command, which launches an external merge tool (like meld, kdiff3, or vimdiff) to help you resolve conflicts in a graphical interface.

Setting Up git mergetool

Before using git mergetool, you need to configure your preferred merge tool. You can set up your default merge tool by running the following command:

bash

git config --global merge.tool <tool-name>

For example, if you prefer using meld as your merge tool, run:

bash

git config --global merge.tool meld

Using git mergetool

Once you've configured your merge tool, you can launch the merge tool to resolve conflicts by running:

bash

git mergetool

Git will open the merge tool and display the conflicting files. Most merge tools will show three panes:

- The **left pane** will display the version from the current branch (the one you're merging into).
- The **right pane** will display the version from the branch being merged.
- The **center pane** is where you can resolve the conflict, combining the changes from both branches as needed.

Once you've resolved all conflicts, save and close the merge tool. Git will then mark the conflicts as resolved and allow you to continue with the merge.

Popular Git Merge Tools

Some commonly used merge tools are:

- **Meld**: A visual diff and merge tool with a simple interface.
- **KDiff3**: A powerful merge tool that can handle three-way merges.

- **P4Merge**: A merge tool from Perforce that works well with Git.
- **VSCode**: The Visual Studio Code editor also provides built-in Git merge tools for conflict resolution.

Merging is one of the most powerful aspects of Git, enabling teams to collaborate on code efficiently. However, handling merge conflicts can be tricky. By understanding how merge conflicts arise and learning advanced conflict resolution strategies, you can streamline your workflow and avoid costly mistakes. Git's three-way merge helps automate much of the conflict resolution, but when things get complicated, tools like git mergetool make it easy to resolve conflicts visually. Whether you're merging code in a solo project or as part of a team, mastering advanced merging techniques in Git is crucial for maintaining a smooth and efficient development process.

CHAPTER 16: SUBMODULES IN GIT

Git submodules are a powerful but often underutilized feature that allow you to include and manage external repositories within your own Git repository. Submodules are particularly useful for projects that depend on external libraries, tools, or other Git repositories, and they allow developers to maintain a consistent history of those dependencies without having to copy their contents directly into the project.

In this chapter, we'll explore what Git submodules are, how to use them, how to manage them, and best practices for keeping submodules in sync with your project. We'll also cover some common issues that developers face when using submodules and how to troubleshoot them effectively.

1. What Are Submodules and When to Use Them?

A Git submodule is essentially a Git repository embedded within another Git repository. You can think of it as a repository inside your repository that keeps its own version history separate from the parent project. This allows you to include external libraries or dependencies within your project without incorporating the actual content directly into your repository.

Use Cases for Submodules

Submodules are most useful in scenarios where you want to include a separate project or library that's developed and maintained independently, but you still want to keep track of the specific version or commit of that project within your own repository. Some common use cases include:

- **Including external libraries**: If you're working on a project that depends on an open-source library or a third-party tool, you can add that project as a submodule rather than copying its code into your repository. This ensures you always have access to the latest updates without losing track of the version you're using.

- **Modularizing code**: For large, modular codebases, submodules allow you to break your project into smaller, more manageable parts, each stored in its own Git repository. This makes collaboration easier, as different teams can work on different submodules independently.

- **Maintaining versioned dependencies**: If your project depends on a specific commit or version of an external repository, using a submodule ensures you always reference the correct version, avoiding potential compatibility issues that could arise from using the latest version of a library.

2. Adding, Updating, and Removing Submodules

a. Adding a Submodule

To add a submodule to your project, you use the git submodule add command. This command takes the URL of the external repository you want to include, as well as the directory where you want to place it in your project.

bash

git submodule add <repository-url> <submodule-directory>
For example, if you want to add a submodule called example-lib:

bash

git submodule add https://github.com/example/example-lib.git external/example-lib
This command does several things:

- It clones the external repository into the specified directory (external/example-lib in this case).
- It creates a new file called .gitmodules, which contains metadata about the submodule, including the repository URL and the directory where it's placed.
- It stages the .gitmodules file and the submodule directory for commit.

b. Initializing and Updating Submodules
When you clone a repository that contains submodules, the submodules themselves are not cloned by default. Instead, you need to initialize and update them using the following commands:

bash

git submodule init

git submodule update

This fetches the submodule's content and checks out the correct commit as referenced by the parent repository.

Alternatively, you can combine both commands into one by running:

bash

git submodule update --init

If you want to ensure that the submodules are always up-to-date when cloning a new repository, you can use the --recursive flag when cloning:

bash

git clone --recursive <repository-url>

c. Updating Submodules

When the parent repository references a new commit in a submodule, or if you want to update the submodule to the latest commit in its repository, you can run the following command within the submodule directory:

bash

git submodule update --remote

This will fetch the latest changes from the submodule's repository and check out the new commit referenced by the parent repository. You can also specify a particular submodule to update if you have multiple submodules:

bash

git submodule update --remote <submodule-name>

d. Removing a Submodule

To remove a submodule from your repository, you need to follow several steps to cleanly remove all traces of the submodule:

1. **Remove the submodule from the .gitmodules file**: Edit the .gitmodules file and delete the entry corresponding to the submodule.

2. **Remove the submodule directory**: Run the following command to remove the submodule directory from the working directory:

   bash

   git rm --cached <submodule-directory>

   This removes the submodule from the index but leaves the actual directory intact. If you want to completely remove the submodule, you can also delete the submodule directory manually.

3. **Commit the changes**: After removing the submodule, commit the changes to remove it from the repository:

bash

git commit -m "Removed submodule <submodule-name>"

4. **Delete the submodule's repository** (optional): If you no longer need the submodule's repository on your local machine, you can safely delete its files. You can also remove any remaining submodule references from the .gitmodules file and .git/config.

3. Best Practices for Managing Submodules

While submodules can be incredibly useful, they come with a few challenges, especially when working in teams or managing multiple submodules. Here are some best practices to help you manage them more effectively:

a. Use Submodules for Versioned Dependencies

Submodules are ideal for managing versioned dependencies. If you rely on a particular version of an external repository, always specify the exact commit you want to reference rather than the latest commit. This ensures that everyone working on the project has access to the same version of the submodule and reduces the risk of compatibility issues.

b. Keep Submodules Updated

It's essential to regularly update the submodules to incorporate any new changes or bug fixes. However, be mindful of when and how you update, as updating a submodule could introduce breaking changes in your project. Always test the changes after updating a submodule.

c. Make Submodule Changes Explicit

If you need to make changes to a submodule, do so explicitly within the submodule itself and push those changes to the submodule's repository. Avoid making changes directly to the submodule directory within the parent repository unless it's necessary for the build process.

d. Use Submodule Branches Sparingly

If you need to use a specific branch within a submodule, be cautious. Submodules usually reference a specific commit, but sometimes it might be tempting to track a branch. If you do this, make sure to consistently check for updates to that branch and sync the submodule accordingly. This can add complexity and potentially lead to issues with merge conflicts.

e. Keep .gitmodules in Sync

The .gitmodules file should always be kept in sync with the submodule directory. Any changes to submodules (such as adding new submodules, removing them, or changing their URL) should also be reflected in this file.

4. Troubleshooting Common Submodule Issues

Submodules can introduce some unique issues, especially when working in a team or with multiple submodules. Here are some common problems you may encounter and how to troubleshoot them:

a. Submodule Not Cloning Properly

If a submodule isn't cloned properly, the most likely issue is that you forgot to initialize or update the submodules after cloning the repository. You can fix this by running:

bash

git submodule update --init --recursive

This ensures that all submodules are initialized and up-to-date.

b. Submodule Changes Not Reflected

If you've made changes to a submodule but they're not showing up in the parent repository, ensure that you've committed and pushed the changes to the submodule repository. After that, update the parent repository to reference the new commit.

bash

git submodule update --remote

Then commit and push the updated submodule reference in the parent repository:

bash

git commit -m "Updated submodule to latest commit"

c. Submodule Conflict During Merge

Submodule conflicts can arise if different branches of the parent repository reference different commits or versions of the submodule. This can be resolved by checking out the correct version of the submodule after resolving any merge conflicts:

bash

git submodule update --init --recursive

If necessary, resolve conflicts in the submodule directory just as you would in any other file.

Git submodules are an incredibly powerful feature for managing external repositories and dependencies in your project. While they come with a learning curve and some management overhead, they can greatly improve your workflow when used properly. By understanding how to add, update, remove, and troubleshoot submodules, you can leverage this feature to keep your project organized and modular. Submodules are particularly useful in large, complex projects where you need to reference other repositories while maintaining clean, versioned dependencies. Follow best practices for managing submodules, and you'll avoid many of the common pitfalls associated with their use.

CHAPTER 17: BEST PRACTICES FOR COMMIT MESSAGES

Commit messages are one of the most important aspects of maintaining a clean and effective Git repository. They serve as a history of your project's evolution, documenting the rationale behind each change and helping team members (and your future self) understand why certain decisions were made. Properly crafted commit messages not only improve project documentation but also enhance collaboration and troubleshooting within teams.

In this chapter, we'll explore why commit messages matter, how to write effective commit messages, and some best practices that you can follow to keep your project's history clear, consistent, and easy to navigate. We'll also cover the importance of using conventions like the imperative mood and conventional commit formats, which can improve both the readability and structure of your Git history.

1. Why Commit Messages Matter

Commit messages are much more than just a log of changes made to a repository. They are a critical part of your project's communication. Here's why they matter:

a. Clarity for Future Developers

Commit messages provide valuable context about what was changed and why. When reviewing a commit, you should be able to understand not only the change itself but also the reasoning behind it. This is especially important in collaborative projects, where multiple developers are working on the same codebase.

Clear commit messages reduce confusion and help other team members grasp the intent behind your changes.

b. Troubleshooting and Debugging

When things go wrong, commit messages become a key part of the debugging process. If you need to identify when a bug was introduced, or if you need to roll back a problematic change, a good commit message can help you pinpoint the exact commit where an issue started. Without meaningful commit messages, this task becomes more difficult and time-consuming.

c. Efficient Collaboration

In a team environment, commit messages allow developers to understand each other's work. Good messages ensure that everyone knows the purpose of a change and the functionality it affects. This is essential in projects that involve regular merging, as it provides context for resolving conflicts or understanding the scope of changes from multiple developers.

d. Tracking Project Progress

Commit messages are an important part of documenting the project's progression over time. When you look back at your project history, well-written messages help you understand the evolution of the codebase, including what features were added, what bugs were fixed, and how the project moved toward its current state.

2. Writing Effective Commit Messages

The goal of a commit message is to be as clear and informative as possible, providing all the necessary context without overwhelming the reader with too much information. There are a few principles to follow to ensure your commit messages are effective:

a. Be Concise but Descriptive

The message should be succinct but provide enough detail to explain the purpose of the change. A good rule of thumb is to summarize the change in one sentence in the subject line and, if necessary, provide further explanation in the body of the message.

Example of a good commit message:

csharp

Fix issue with login form validation

If the change is complex or requires more context, the body of the commit message can elaborate:

css

Fix issue with login form validation

The form was not correctly validating email addresses. Added regular expression to check email format and added error handling to display messages to the user.

b. Explain "Why", Not Just "What"

It's often obvious what the code change is by looking at the diff, but it's not always clear **why** the change was made. Whenever possible, explain the reasoning behind your changes. This can save a lot of time when looking back at a commit months later.

Example:

Instead of writing:

Fix bug in registration page
You can write:

vbnet

Fix bug in registration page where users could not sign up with email addresses containing special characters

The issue was caused by incorrect validation in the email input field. Updated the regex to allow valid special characters and added more comprehensive test cases.

c. Use a Consistent Format

Establishing a consistent format for commit messages makes your project's history easier to read and navigate. Developers often follow some standard conventions for consistency and clarity. A well-known convention is to use a **short, imperative subject line** followed by a more detailed body if needed.

3. Following the "Imperative Mood" Rule

One key convention in writing commit messages is the use of the **imperative mood**. This means writing the message as if you are giving a command or instruction. For example, instead of writing:

- "Fixed the bug in login form"
- "Fixing issue with form validation"

Write:

- "Fix bug in login form"
- "Add validation to email input field"

The imperative mood is preferred because it matches the behavior of Git itself. When you use git commit, it records the changes as though you are telling Git to "apply this change" or "fix this issue."

Why Imperative Mood Makes Sense

- **Consistency**: It standardizes commit messages, making them easier to read.

- **Clarity**: It's direct and to the point.

- **Git's Internal Commit Structure**: Git logs commit messages as if they are commands. Using the imperative mood aligns with this internal structure, making the history easier to interpret and more consistent.

4. Using Conventional Commit Formats for Consistency

In large teams and open-source projects, consistency in commit messages is crucial. One widely adopted convention is **Conventional Commits**. This standard provides a structured format for writing commit messages, making it easier to automate tasks like versioning, changelog generation, and continuous integration.

a. Basic Structure of a Conventional Commit

The general structure for a conventional commit is as follows:

php

```
<type>(<scope>): <subject>
```

- **type**: A one-word identifier for the type of change (e.g., feat, fix, docs, style, etc.).

- **scope**: An optional part that indicates the area of the code affected (e.g., login, auth, ui). This is useful for large projects to quickly understand where the change occurred.
- **subject**: A short description of what was done, written in the imperative mood.

b. Types of Commits

Here are the most common commit types used in conventional commit formats:

- **feat**: A new feature or functionality.
  - Example: feat(user-auth): add password reset feature
- **fix**: A bug fix.
  - Example: fix(button): correct button alignment on mobile devices
- **docs**: Documentation changes.
  - Example: docs(readme): update installation instructions
- **style**: Changes that affect the style (e.g., formatting, missing semicolons).
  - Example: style(code): fix inconsistent indentation
- **refactor**: Code changes that neither fix a bug nor add a feature but improve code structure or readability.
  - Example: refactor(auth): simplify login logic
- **test**: Adding or updating tests.

o   Example: test(api): add unit test for authentication

- **chore**: Routine tasks that don't affect the code (e.g., build tools, dependencies).

    o   Example: chore(deps): update dependency lodash to version 4.17.21

c. Examples of Conventional Commit Messages

- feat(auth): implement multi-factor authentication
- fix(ui): resolve issue with dropdown menu not closing
- docs(contributing): update guidelines for submitting pull requests
- style(css): fix font size in navbar
- chore(build): update webpack configuration

d. Benefits of Using Conventional Commits

1. **Automatic Changelog Generation**: With consistent commit types, tools like standard-version can automatically generate changelogs based on commit history.
2. **Semantic Versioning**: Tools can use commit types to automate versioning. For example, a feat commit may trigger a major version bump, while a fix commit triggers a minor version bump.
3. **Improved Collaboration**: When everyone follows the same format, it's easier to understand the history of

changes in the codebase, which is especially valuable when working in large teams or open-source projects.

5. Summary of Best Practices

Here's a quick summary of the best practices for writing commit messages:

- **Be concise but descriptive**: Provide enough detail so others can understand why the change was made, but keep the message short and to the point.
- **Explain "why" the change was made**: If possible, provide context for the change to make it clear why the change was necessary.
- **Use the imperative mood**: Write commit messages as if you are giving an order (e.g., "Fix bug" instead of "Fixed bug").
- **Follow a consistent format**: Use a standardized structure, such as conventional commits, to ensure your commit messages are easy to understand and automate.
- **Use the body of the message for additional context**: If necessary, provide more detailed explanations in the body of the commit message to clarify the scope or reasoning behind the change.

- **Commit often and with clarity**: Small, focused commits are easier to review and understand. Aim to make commits that address a single issue or feature.

Commit messages may seem like a small part of the development process, but they have a significant impact on the maintainability of your codebase, especially in collaborative environments. By following the best practices outlined in this chapter, you can ensure that your commit history is clear, informative, and consistent. This will make it easier for you and your team to manage your project, debug issues, and maintain high-quality code over time.

CHAPTER 18: MANAGING LARGE REPOSITORIES AND FILES

As your projects grow in size and complexity, managing large repositories and files in Git can become a challenging task. Git was designed for managing source code, but when your repository includes large binary files, media assets, or datasets, Git can struggle with performance. This chapter covers strategies for managing large repositories and files in Git, including techniques for efficiently cloning large repositories, using Git Large File Storage (LFS) for binary files, and best practices for maintaining performance in a growing codebase.

1. Strategies for Handling Large Files in Git

Git excels in managing text-based files, such as source code, because it uses a highly efficient versioning system based on diffs (differences between file versions). However, this approach is not ideal for large binary files like images, videos, compiled binaries, or large datasets. Binary files do not have meaningful diffs, meaning Git will track the entire file each time it changes, which leads to repository bloat and performance issues.

Here are some strategies for dealing with large files:

a. Avoid Storing Large Binary Files Directly in Git

The first strategy is to avoid committing large binary files directly to the Git repository. Storing large files in Git increases the repository size, which slows down common operations like cloning, pulling, and pushing. Binary files also increase the risk of repository fragmentation, as Git has to store multiple copies of the entire file for every change.

Instead, use a separate file storage solution that integrates with Git, such as:

- **External file storage (e.g., cloud services)**: Store large files in cloud storage systems like Amazon S3, Google Cloud Storage, or Dropbox and reference the files in the repository. This approach works well for assets like images or videos that do not change frequently.
- **Git LFS (Large File Storage)**: This is a more Git-native approach that allows you to store large files in a separate system while keeping track of their versions within Git.

b. Use Git Submodules for Large Files or External Projects

Git submodules allow you to keep large files or other repositories in a separate Git repository and reference them as part of your main repository. This is useful for managing third-party libraries, large assets, or other external dependencies without cluttering your main repository. However, submodules come with their own set of challenges, such as managing submodule updates and ensuring that all contributors are aware of the submodule setup.

2. Using Git LFS (Large File Storage) for Binary Files

Git Large File Storage (LFS) is an extension to Git that allows you to manage large binary files more efficiently by replacing them with lightweight pointers in the Git repository. The actual file content is stored separately in a different server or storage system.

a. How Git LFS Works

When you use Git LFS, large files are replaced with pointers (small text files that contain metadata, including the file size and location). The actual files are stored on a dedicated LFS server or service (e.g., GitHub's LFS service). When you clone or pull a repository, Git fetches the large files from the LFS server automatically.

For example, when you add an image to a repository using Git LFS, it will store a pointer to the image file in the Git repository, but the image itself is stored on a separate server. This means Git only tracks changes to the pointer file and avoids bloating the repository with large binary data.

b. Setting Up Git LFS

Here's how you can set up Git LFS:

1. **Install Git LFS:**
   - For macOS: brew install git-lfs
   - For Windows: Download and install Git LFS from https://git-lfs.github.com/
   - For Linux: Use the package manager specific to your distribution (e.g., sudo apt-get install git-lfs for Ubuntu).

2. **Initialize Git LFS:**

   Run the following command to set up Git LFS in your repository:

   bash

   git lfs install

3. **Track Large Files:**

   To track a specific type of file (e.g., .mp4 files), run the following command:

   bash

git lfs track "*.mp4"

This tells Git LFS to track all .mp4 files in your repository. The *.mp4 pattern can be adjusted for any file type (e.g., .zip, .jpg, etc.).

4. **Add, Commit, and Push Large Files:**

After tracking the file types, you can add, commit, and push large files as you normally would. Git LFS will handle the storage of the files:

bash

git add my_large_file.mp4
git commit -m "Add large file"
git push origin main

When you push to the repository, Git LFS uploads the actual file to the LFS server, while Git only tracks the pointer file.

5. **Cloning a Repository with Git LFS:**

When cloning a repository that uses Git LFS, the large files will automatically be fetched after cloning the repository:

bash

git clone https://github.com/myrepo.git

This will download both the repository and the associated large files from the LFS server.

c. Git LFS Considerations

- **Storage Costs**: Git LFS storage is typically offered by Git hosting providers, such as GitHub, GitLab, or Bitbucket. However, it often comes with a limited free tier, and large repositories may incur additional storage or bandwidth fees.

- **Performance Impact**: While Git LFS can significantly improve the performance of large repositories, accessing large files may still be slower than text-based files. Always consider the nature of your files and whether LFS is the right choice for your project.

3. Cloning Large Repositories Efficiently

Cloning a large Git repository can take a significant amount of time and disk space, especially when the repository contains large files. Here are some strategies to clone large repositories efficiently:

a. Shallow Clone

A shallow clone is a clone of a repository with a limited history. Instead of fetching the entire commit history, you only download the most recent commits. This can reduce the amount of data transferred and speed up the cloning process.

Use the --depth flag to specify the number of commits you want to clone:

bash

git clone --depth 1 https://github.com/myrepo.git

This will clone only the latest commit. If you need more history, you can increase the depth (e.g., --depth 10 for the last 10 commits).

b. Sparse Checkout

Sparse checkout allows you to clone a repository but only check out specific files or directories. This can be especially useful when you're only interested in a subset of the repository's content and don't need the entire codebase.

To enable sparse checkout:

1. Clone the repository as usual:

    bash

    git clone https://github.com/myrepo.git
    cd myrepo

2. Enable sparse checkout:

    bash

git sparse-checkout init --cone

3. Specify the directories or files you want to check out:

bash

git sparse-checkout set path/to/directory

This will only check out the specified files, reducing the amount of data you need to download.

4. Managing Repository Size and Performance

As your repository grows, it's important to regularly monitor and manage its size to maintain performance. Here are a few strategies:

a. Prune Unused References

Git can accumulate stale references, especially after you've removed branches or tags. Use the following command to clean up unnecessary references:

bash

git gc --prune=now

This command will remove old, unused references and help optimize the repository's performance.

b. Use Git Hooks to Prevent Large Files from Being Added

One proactive approach to managing repository size is to use Git hooks to prevent large files from being added to the repository in the first place. For example, you can set up a pre-commit hook that rejects large files or files above a certain size limit.

c. Monitor Repository Size

Git hosting services like GitHub provide tools to monitor the size of your repository. Keep an eye on the size and ensure that it doesn't grow too large. If the repository size becomes unmanageable, consider splitting it into smaller repositories or moving large assets to external storage.

Managing large repositories and files in Git requires careful consideration and planning. By using strategies like Git LFS for binary files, shallow clones for efficient repository cloning, and sparse checkout for selective file access, you can keep your repository performing well, even as it grows in size. Regularly cleaning up your repository and monitoring its size will ensure that your Git workflow remains efficient and manageable.

CHAPTER 19: SECURITY AND AUTHENTICATION IN GITHUB

As GitHub becomes an increasingly popular platform for software development, understanding and implementing security best practices is crucial for safeguarding both your code and personal data. GitHub provides several mechanisms to ensure secure authentication, control access, and protect your account from unauthorized access. This chapter will guide you through the best practices for securing your GitHub account, managing authentication methods, and ensuring that your repositories and contributions remain secure.

1. Using SSH Keys for Secure Authentication

a. What Are SSH Keys?

SSH (Secure Shell) keys are a pair of cryptographic keys used for secure communication between your local machine and remote servers, including GitHub. An SSH key pair consists of a **private key** (which you keep secure on your computer) and a **public key** (which you share with GitHub). When you use SSH for authentication, GitHub verifies your identity by matching your public key to your private key, eliminating the need to enter a password each time you push or pull from a repository.

Using SSH keys instead of HTTP/HTTPS for authentication provides several benefits:

- **Enhanced Security**: SSH keys are more secure than passwords because they are much harder to brute-force.
- **Convenience**: Once set up, SSH keys allow you to authenticate automatically without entering your GitHub username and password every time.
- **Integration with other services**: Many CI/CD pipelines, deployment tools, and other automation tools use SSH keys for secure authentication.

b. Generating and Adding SSH Keys

Here are the steps to set up SSH keys for GitHub:

1. **Generate SSH Key Pair**:

   Open your terminal and use the following command to generate a new SSH key pair:

   bash

ssh-keygen -t rsa -b 4096 -C "your_email@example.com"

This command creates a new RSA key pair with a 4096-bit key length and associates it with your GitHub email address. Follow the prompts to save the key and set a passphrase (optional, but recommended for additional security).

2. **Add Your SSH Key to the SSH Agent**:

To ensure your key is loaded into the SSH agent (which manages your SSH keys), run the following command:

bash

eval "$(ssh-agent -s)"

Then, add your newly generated key to the agent:

bash

ssh-add ~/.ssh/id_rsa

3. **Add Your SSH Key to GitHub**:

Copy your public key to your clipboard with the following command:

bash

cat ~/.ssh/id_rsa.pub

Now, go to your GitHub account settings:

- o Navigate to **Settings** > **SSH and GPG keys** > **New SSH key**.
- o Paste your public key in the key field, give it a title (e.g., "Personal Laptop"), and click **Add SSH key**.

4. **Test the Connection**:

To verify that everything is working correctly, run the following command:

bash

ssh -T git@github.com

You should receive a success message, confirming that you've successfully authenticated via SSH.

2. Two-Factor Authentication (2FA) on GitHub

a. What is Two-Factor Authentication?

Two-Factor Authentication (2FA) is an added layer of security that requires you to provide two pieces of information to verify your identity:

1. **Something you know** (your password)
2. **Something you have** (a code sent to your phone or generated by an app)

2FA helps protect your GitHub account from unauthorized access, even if your password is compromised. GitHub offers multiple methods for setting up 2FA, such as using an authentication app or receiving codes via SMS.

b. Setting Up Two-Factor Authentication on GitHub

To enable 2FA on your GitHub account:

1. **Navigate to Settings**:
   o Go to your GitHub account and click on your profile picture in the top right corner.
   o Click **Settings**.
2. **Enable Two-Factor Authentication**:
   o In the left sidebar, select **Security**.
   o Under the **Two-factor authentication** section, click **Enable two-factor authentication**.
   o GitHub will guide you through the setup process. You will need to use an authentication app (such as Google Authenticator, Authy, or 1Password) to scan a QR code and generate time-based one-time passwords (TOTP).

3. **Backup Codes**: After enabling 2FA, GitHub will provide you with a set of backup codes. These codes can be used if you lose access to your primary 2FA method (e.g., if you lose your phone). It's important to store these backup codes in a safe place.

4. **Test Your Setup**: Once enabled, GitHub will require you to enter a code from your authentication app each time you log in or perform actions that require authentication (like pushing to a repository).

c. Using Personal Access Tokens (PATs) with 2FA

If you've enabled 2FA, GitHub no longer allows you to authenticate via your GitHub password when pushing to repositories or accessing the API. Instead, you must use a **Personal Access Token** (PAT).

3. Managing Personal Access Tokens

a. What are Personal Access Tokens?

A Personal Access Token (PAT) is a secure way to authenticate with GitHub over HTTPS. It serves as an alternative to your GitHub password, particularly when 2FA is enabled. PATs are recommended for interacting with the GitHub API, automation tools, and Git clients. They offer a higher level of security than using your password directly, as they can be scoped to specific actions and can be revoked at any time.

b. Creating a Personal Access Token

1. **Navigate to Settings**:
   o Go to your GitHub account settings and click **Developer settings > Personal access tokens**.

2. **Generate a Token**:
   o Click **Generate new token**.
   o Provide a description (e.g., "GitHub CLI access").
   o Select the **scopes** (permissions) for the token. Scopes determine what actions the token can perform, such as reading repository data, pushing commits, or managing issues.
   o Click **Generate token**.

3. **Store the Token Securely**:
   o Once the token is generated, **copy it immediately** and store it in a secure place. You won't be able to see it again.
   o You can now use the token in place of your GitHub password for operations like git push or when accessing the GitHub API.

c. Revoking and Managing Tokens

You can revoke or regenerate tokens at any time from the **Personal access tokens** settings page. If you suspect that a token has been compromised, it's good practice to revoke it immediately and issue a new one.

4. Best Practices for Securing Your GitHub Account

Securing your GitHub account is not just about using strong authentication methods; it's about adopting good practices that help safeguard your account, repositories, and data. Below are some best practices to follow:

a. Use Strong, Unique Passwords

While GitHub provides multiple authentication methods, your password is still the first line of defense. Make sure to:

- Use a strong password (at least 12 characters, with a mix of letters, numbers, and symbols).
- Avoid using the same password across multiple services.
- Use a password manager to securely store and manage your passwords.

b. Enable 2FA Everywhere

Enable 2FA on your GitHub account, as well as on any associated services (e.g., your email account). Even if your password is compromised, the second factor will provide an additional layer of security.

c. Be Cautious with Third-Party Integrations

Many developers integrate GitHub with third-party tools, like continuous integration/continuous deployment (CI/CD) platforms, project management tools, and code quality checkers. Be cautious about what permissions you grant to these tools, and regularly review the authorized OAuth apps on your GitHub account.

- In **Settings** > **Applications**, you can view and revoke third-party applications that have access to your GitHub account.

d. Review and Manage Collaborators and Teams

If you manage a repository or an organization on GitHub, carefully manage who has access to your codebase:

- Use **least privilege**: Only grant the necessary permissions to collaborators.
- Regularly review and audit collaborators and team members.

e. Monitor Your GitHub Security Settings

Regularly check your security settings in GitHub. This includes ensuring 2FA is enabled, reviewing access tokens, and monitoring for any unusual login activity. You can view your **security advisories**, which notify you of potential vulnerabilities in your dependencies, and monitor for any suspicious activity in your account's security logs.

f. Backup Important Data

GitHub generally offers good availability and redundancy, but it's always a good idea to keep backup copies of your important repositories. This is especially true for private or critical repositories that you cannot afford to lose. Consider mirroring your repositories to a local or external server.

Securing your GitHub account and repositories is essential in today's development environment, where sensitive data and proprietary code are often stored in the cloud. By using secure authentication methods like SSH keys and 2FA, and by adopting good practices like using Personal Access Tokens and reviewing third-party integrations, you can significantly reduce the risk of unauthorized access to your codebase. Always stay vigilant and proactive in maintaining the security of your GitHub account, and encourage your team to do the same.

CHAPTER 20: ADVANCED GITHUB FEATURES

GitHub is much more than just a platform for hosting code. It offers a wide range of advanced features that can help streamline your development process, enhance collaboration, and automate workflows. In this chapter, we'll explore some of GitHub's more powerful tools that can be leveraged to manage projects, track issues, automate deployment, and improve the overall organization of your codebase.

1. Issues, Labels, and Milestones

a. What Are Issues?

GitHub Issues are used to track tasks, bugs, feature requests, and other work items related to your project. Issues can be created for anything that needs attention within the repository, and they serve as a central point of communication for the development team.

Each issue can have a title, description, assignees, and labels to categorize and prioritize the work. They can also include milestones, comments, and references to commits and pull requests (PRs), making them a crucial tool for tracking the progress of a project.

b. Labels

Labels in GitHub are a way to categorize issues and pull requests for easier tracking and filtering. Labels help you group similar issues together, such as:

- bug: Used to identify bugs.
- enhancement: Used to mark requests for new features.
- priority: Labels like high, medium, or low to set the priority of an issue.
- help wanted: Indicates that someone else can assist with the issue.
- good first issue: Designed for beginners to help get started with contributions.

How to Add Labels:

1. Open an issue or pull request.
2. On the right-hand side, under **Labels**, click the "gear" icon.
3. Select from the pre-existing labels or create new ones to apply them.

Using labels consistently across your issues will help provide structure, making it easier to find and prioritize tasks.

c. Milestones

Milestones are used to track the progress of a group of issues that are related to a specific goal, such as a software release or a project phase. They provide a high-level overview of the progress made toward that goal.

How to Use Milestones:

1. Open an issue.
2. On the right sidebar, find the **Milestone** section.
3. Either choose an existing milestone or create a new one to associate the issue with a milestone.
4. As you progress through issues, milestones automatically update to reflect completion status.

Milestones also provide an overall progress bar, giving you a clear view of how far along the project is and how many issues are remaining.

2. Managing GitHub Projects for Project Management

GitHub Projects offers a project management feature that integrates with issues, pull requests, and other GitHub activities to help organize and manage workflows.

a. What is GitHub Projects?

GitHub Projects allows you to create Kanban-style boards within your repository to track work items. This feature helps you manage your workflow visually, providing an easy way to organize tasks, bugs, features, and other work items. You can create multiple projects for different areas or phases of your work.

b. Creating a Project Board

1. **Navigate to the Repository**:
   - Go to the repository where you want to create the project.

2. **Create a New Project**:
   - In the repository's main page, click on the **Projects** tab.
   - Click **New Project** and choose a template or start with a blank board.

3. **Set Up Columns**:
   - Columns in a project board represent different stages of the workflow (e.g., To Do, In Progress, Done).

- o You can create and customize columns based on your workflow needs.

4. **Add Issues and Pull Requests**:
   - o Drag and drop issues and pull requests from the repository onto the project board.
   - o This allows you to visually track the status of tasks across multiple columns.

c. Using Automation in Projects

GitHub Projects allows you to automate certain actions based on triggers, such as moving issues between columns when they are closed, opened, or labeled. This can save time and ensure that your board stays up to date.

For Example:

- **"When a pull request is merged, move the issue to "Done."**
- **"Automatically assign the bug label when an issue is marked with "high priority."**

Automating these workflows can reduce manual work and improve consistency across your team.

3. GitHub Actions for CI/CD Workflows

a. What Are GitHub Actions?

GitHub Actions is a powerful automation tool integrated directly into GitHub that enables you to automate workflows for software development. It's commonly used for Continuous Integration/Continuous Deployment (CI/CD) pipelines, but it can also automate many other tasks such as testing, building, linting, deployment, and much more.

GitHub Actions uses workflows, which are custom automated processes defined by YAML files that are stored in the .github/workflows directory of your repository. These workflows are triggered by specific events such as pushes to a branch, pull requests, or manual triggers.

b. Setting Up a Basic CI/CD Pipeline

1. **Create a Workflow File**: In your repository, create a .github/workflows directory, and inside it, create a .yml file (e.g., ci.yml) for your workflow.

2. **Define Workflow Events**: Specify which events will trigger the workflow (e.g., a push to the main branch):

yaml

name: CI Pipeline

on:
  push:

branches:

- main

3. **Define Jobs and Steps**: Inside the workflow file, you define jobs and steps. Jobs represent individual tasks that run in parallel, and steps are the individual commands executed within a job. A typical CI pipeline might include steps like checking out the code, setting up dependencies, running tests, and deploying the application.

yaml

```yaml
jobs:
  build:
    runs-on: ubuntu-latest

    steps:
      - name: Checkout Code
        uses: actions/checkout@v2

      - name: Set up Python
        uses: actions/setup-python@v2
        with:
          python-version: '3.x'

      - name: Install Dependencies
```

```
run: pip install -r requirements.txt

- name: Run Tests
  run: pytest
```

4. **Triggering the Workflow**: Once the file is committed to the repository, the workflow will automatically trigger on every push to the main branch. GitHub will provide logs of the workflow's execution, including any successes or failures, allowing you to easily track the status.

c. Benefits of GitHub Actions

- **Automated testing**: Run tests automatically on each commit or pull request to ensure that code changes do not break functionality.
- **Continuous deployment**: Deploy code to production or staging environments whenever changes are merged into a specified branch.
- **Custom workflows**: Create tailored workflows that meet the specific needs of your project, whether it's for linting, building, deploying, or other processes.

GitHub Actions is a powerful tool for automating your software development lifecycle, helping you save time and ensure that your code is always tested and deployed in a consistent manner.

4. Creating and Maintaining a README File

a. Why a README File Matters

The README file is often the first point of contact for users or contributors to your project. A well-written README file can make a big difference in how others perceive your project, and it provides essential information to help users and developers understand what the project is, how to use it, and how to contribute.

A good README should be clear, concise, and include key sections such as:

- **Project Title**: The name of the project.
- **Description**: A brief explanation of what the project does and why it exists.
- **Installation Instructions**: How to set up the project locally.
- **Usage**: How to use the software or tools provided.
- **Contributing Guidelines**: How others can contribute to the project.
- **License**: The licensing terms for the project.
- **Contact Information**: Ways to reach the maintainers.

b. Creating a Basic README

You can create a README.md file in the root of your repository, using Markdown syntax to structure the content. Here's an example of a simple README template:

markdown

Project Name

Description

A brief description of what the project does.

Installation

Steps to install and set up the project locally:

```bash
git clone https://github.com/yourusername/yourproject.git
cd yourproject
npm install
```

USAGE

How to run the project:

bash

```
npm start
```

CONTRIBUTING

We welcome contributions! Please fork the repository and submit pull requests.

LICENSE

MIT License

CONTACT

Your Name - your.email@example.com

vbnet

c. **Maintaining Your README**

As your project evolves, it's important to keep the README file up to date with the latest features, setup instructions, and usage examples. Regularly reviewing and editing your README will ensure that new contributors and users can easily understand and contribute to your project.

Conclusion

Mastering the advanced features of GitHub can significantly improve your development workflow.

CHAPTER 21: GIT AND CONTINUOUS INTEGRATION/CONTINUOUS DEPLOYMENT (CI/CD)

Continuous Integration (CI) and Continuous Deployment (CD) are practices that aim to automate the process of integrating and deploying code changes to improve software development speed and quality. Git, as a version control system, plays a central role in CI/CD workflows by facilitating the management of code changes, branching strategies, and collaboration across teams. In this chapter, we'll explore how Git integrates with CI/CD tools like Jenkins, CircleCI, and GitHub Actions, as well as best practices for automating testing, deployment, and monitoring CI/CD workflows.

1. Integrating Git with CI/CD Tools (Jenkins, CircleCI, GitHub Actions)

a. What is CI/CD?

CI/CD is a combination of practices that enable developers to automate the process of testing, integrating, and deploying code. CI involves frequently merging code changes into a shared repository, with automated tests run to ensure that each change does not introduce errors. CD refers to automatically deploying the code to production or staging environments.

Integrating Git with CI/CD tools allows you to streamline this process and improve software delivery by making it more efficient and error-free.

b. Jenkins Integration

Jenkins is one of the most widely used open-source CI/CD tools, and it can be integrated with Git to automate build, test, and deployment pipelines.

Setting Up Jenkins with Git:

1. **Install Git Plugin in Jenkins**:
   o Go to Jenkins Dashboard > Manage Jenkins > Manage Plugins.
   o Search for "Git Plugin" and install it.
2. **Create a Jenkins Job**:
   o In Jenkins, create a new **Freestyle project**.

- In the **Source Code Management** section, choose **Git** and provide the repository URL (e.g., https://github.com/user/repo.git).
- You can configure the Git repository to be pulled from GitHub, GitLab, or Bitbucket.

3. **Configure Build Triggers**:
   - Set Jenkins to poll the Git repository for changes or trigger builds via webhooks when changes are pushed to the repository.

4. **Add Build Steps**:
   - Configure build steps to automate tasks like running tests (mvn test for Maven, npm test for Node.js), building the application, or deploying it to staging or production.

Advantages of Jenkins:

- Highly customizable.
- Wide community support with numerous plugins.
- Can be used with any Git repository hosting service.

c. CircleCI Integration

CircleCI is a cloud-based CI/CD tool known for its speed and ease of setup. It integrates seamlessly with GitHub repositories and offers powerful configuration via .circleci/config.yml files.

Setting Up CircleCI with GitHub:

1. **Connect CircleCI to GitHub**:

   o Sign up for CircleCI and connect it to your GitHub account.

   o Select the repository you want to integrate and start building.

2. **Create a Configuration File**:

   o In the root of your repository, create a .circleci/config.yml file that contains the CI/CD pipeline configuration.

Example of a simple CircleCI configuration for a Node.js app:

yaml

```yaml
version: 2.1
jobs:
  build:
    docker:
      - image: circleci/python:3.8
    steps:
      - checkout
      - run:
          name: Install dependencies
          command: npm install
      - run:
```

```
    name: Run tests
    command: npm test
  workflows:
   version: 2
   build:
    jobs:
     - build
```

Advantages of CircleCI:

- Easy setup and minimal configuration.
- Fast execution and caching of dependencies for quicker builds.
- Integration with Docker for containerized environments.

d. GitHub Actions Integration

GitHub Actions is a native CI/CD service provided by GitHub, which allows you to automate workflows directly within your GitHub repository. It's powerful and highly customizable with YAML-based configurations.

Setting Up GitHub Actions:

1. **Create a Workflow File**:
   - In your repository, create a .github/workflows directory, then create a .yml file (e.g., ci.yml).
2. **Define the Workflow**:

o In the .yml file, define the event that triggers the workflow (e.g., push to a specific branch) and the steps in the pipeline.

Example of a simple GitHub Actions configuration:

yaml

```yaml
name: Node.js CI

on:
 push:
  branches:
   - main

jobs:
 build:
  runs-on: ubuntu-latest
  steps:
   - name: Checkout code
     uses: actions/checkout@v2
   - name: Set up Node.js
     uses: actions/setup-node@v2
     with:
      node-version: '14'
   - name: Install dependencies
```

run: npm install

- name: Run tests

run: npm test

Advantages of GitHub Actions:

- Directly integrated into GitHub, with no need for third-party services.
- Flexible with matrix builds, conditional steps, and artifact handling.
- Can easily automate tasks like linting, testing, building, and deployment.

2. Automating Testing and Deployment with Git

Automating testing and deployment using Git ensures that code changes are continuously tested, integrated, and deployed with minimal human intervention. This improves software quality and reduces the time spent on manual tasks.

a. Automating Testing

Automated testing ensures that new code changes don't break existing functionality. Tools like Jest, Mocha, and PyTest can be integrated into your CI/CD pipeline to automatically run unit, integration, and end-to-end tests.

- **Unit Tests**: Test individual functions or modules for expected behavior.

- **Integration Tests**: Test how different parts of the system interact with each other.
- **End-to-End Tests**: Test the entire application to ensure all components work together.

Once tests are set up, you can automate their execution in your CI/CD pipeline using tools like Jenkins, CircleCI, or GitHub Actions.

b. Automating Deployment

Automating deployment ensures that code changes are automatically deployed to staging or production environments after passing tests. CI/CD tools can be configured to deploy automatically when changes are pushed to specific branches (e.g., pushing to main deploys to production).

- **Continuous Deployment**: Deploy code automatically whenever a change passes the test suite.
- **Staging Environment**: Deploy to a staging environment first to validate changes before going to production.
- **Rollback Strategy**: Automatically revert to a previous stable version in case of deployment failures.

3. Using Branches in CI/CD Pipelines

Branches in Git are used to separate different features or stages of development, and they play a crucial role in CI/CD pipelines. You can have different workflows for different branches, such as:

- **Development Branches**: CI pipelines trigger on every commit or pull request to the dev branch for testing.
- **Feature Branches**: Individual feature branches can have their own pipeline to run tests and validate changes before merging.
- **Production Branch**: The main or master branch may trigger the deployment process to the production environment.

a. Branch-Based Pipelines:

Most CI/CD tools allow you to define different pipeline configurations based on the branch being worked on. For example:

- Push to feature/* branches triggers tests.
- Push to main branch triggers deployment.

Example in GitHub Actions:

yaml

on:
 push:
  branches:

- main

- 'feature/*'

b. Feature Toggles:

Feature toggles can be used in conjunction with branches to ensure that unfinished features don't disrupt production workflows. The CI/CD system can deploy a feature to production but keep it inactive until it's ready to be enabled.

4. Monitoring and Debugging CI/CD Workflows

Once your CI/CD pipeline is in place, it's essential to monitor the workflows and ensure they are running smoothly. This includes checking for build failures, slow test executions, and deployment issues.

a. Monitoring Builds and Deployments

CI/CD tools provide detailed logs for each build and deployment, allowing you to trace any issues that arise. Tools like Jenkins, CircleCI, and GitHub Actions provide dashboards that display the status of recent builds, test results, and deployment success.

- **Notifications**: Configure notifications (via email, Slack, etc.) for failed builds or deployments.
- **Artifacts**: Store build artifacts (e.g., logs, test results) for later inspection.

b. Debugging Build Failures

When a build or deployment fails, you'll need to investigate the logs and identify the root cause. Common issues include:

- **Dependency issues**: Missing or incorrect dependencies.
- **Test failures**: Code changes that break existing functionality.
- **Deployment problems**: Environment configuration issues or incorrect deployment steps.

Use tools like **git bisect** to track down which commit caused the issue, and **git revert** to roll back problematic changes.

Integrating Git with CI/CD tools such as Jenkins, CircleCI, and GitHub Actions allows for faster, more efficient, and reliable software development. By automating testing, deployment, and monitoring workflows, developers can focus more on writing code and less on manual tasks. Understanding how to work with branches in CI/CD, use automated deployment strategies, and debug issues as they arise ensures that your software is always up-to-date, tested, and ready for production. By mastering CI/CD, you're setting your team up for success in delivering high-quality software faster and more reliably.

CHAPTER 22: HANDLING MERGE CONFLICTS EFFICIENTLY

Merge conflicts are a common challenge in collaborative software development. They occur when multiple developers make changes to the same part of a file or when Git is unable to automatically reconcile differences between branches. Effective handling of merge conflicts is essential for maintaining smooth collaboration and a clean codebase. In this chapter, we'll explore how to identify, resolve, and prevent merge conflicts in Git.

1. Understanding the Different Types of Merge Conflicts

Merge conflicts arise when Git cannot automatically reconcile changes made in two different branches. There are several scenarios in which this can occur, including:

a. Conflicting Changes on the Same Line

When two branches modify the same line of a file, Git is unable to decide which change to keep. This is one of the most common types of merge conflicts.

Example:

- In **branch A**, a developer changes the content of line 45 in a file.
- In **branch B**, another developer also changes the same line, but in a different way.

When merging the two branches, Git will flag the conflict because it cannot automatically decide which version of the line to keep.

b. Conflicting Changes to the Same File but Different Lines

Git can usually handle changes to different lines in the same file, but if two branches modify different sections in the same file (but in an incompatible way), a conflict may occur. This might happen in large files with many modifications.

Example:

- In **branch A**, a developer modifies lines 20–30.
- In **branch B**, another developer modifies lines 50–60.

If these changes involve structural alterations that conflict, such as different variable names or functions being refactored, Git will mark this as a conflict.

c. Conflicts with File Renaming or Deletion

Conflicts may arise if one branch renames or deletes a file that the other branch has modified. In such cases, Git will need the developer to specify whether to keep the file, rename it, or delete it.

Example:

- In **branch A**, a developer deletes file1.txt.
- In **branch B**, another developer modifies file1.txt.

Git cannot determine whether to keep or delete the file without user input.

2. Tools for Conflict Resolution

There are several tools and strategies that can help resolve merge conflicts in Git. Here are some of the most commonly used options:

a. Git's Built-in Conflict Markers

When a conflict occurs, Git will add conflict markers in the affected file(s). These markers highlight the conflicting changes, and you'll need to manually edit the file to decide which changes to keep.

Conflict Markers Example:

diff

<<<<<<< HEAD
This is the content from the current branch.
=======
This is the content from the branch you are merging.
>>>>>>> feature-branch

- <<<<<<< **HEAD**: The section from the current branch.
- =======: A separator between the conflicting changes.
- >>>>>>> **feature-branch**: The section from the branch being merged.

To resolve the conflict, you need to manually edit the file to remove the conflict markers and decide which content to keep, or merge the changes together if necessary.

b. Merge Tools and Editors

Many Git clients (both GUI and command-line) integrate with visual merge tools that make it easier to identify and resolve conflicts. Some popular merge tools include:

- **KDiff3**: A graphical diff and merge tool that shows the differences between files and allows you to merge changes visually.
- **Meld**: A simple, visual diff tool that can help compare files and directories.
- **P4Merge**: A free visual tool from Perforce, useful for resolving complex conflicts.
- **GitKraken**: A popular Git GUI with an integrated merge conflict resolution tool.
- **VS Code**: Integrated Git support in Visual Studio Code allows you to see and resolve conflicts directly within the editor.

These tools often display a side-by-side comparison of the conflicting changes, making it easier to understand and resolve them.

c. Command-Line Tools

Git provides command-line tools to help with conflict resolution. For example:

- **git diff**: Shows the differences between your working directory and the index, which can be useful in understanding what changes are conflicting.
- **git mergetool**: Invokes a merge tool to help you resolve conflicts using the external editor of your choice (e.g., KDiff3, Meld).
- **git status**: Displays the status of the merge, including any files that are in a conflicted state.

3. Using Conflict Markers to Manage Merges

When a conflict happens, Git marks the file as "unmerged" and adds conflict markers to indicate where the differences occur. To manage merges efficiently:

a. Step-by-Step Conflict Resolution Process

1. **Check for Conflicts**: Run git status to identify which files have conflicts.

   bash

   git status
   This will list files in the "unmerged" state.

2. **Open the Conflicted Files**: Open the files with conflicts in your preferred editor. You will see the conflict markers and the conflicting changes from each branch.

3. **Manually Resolve the Conflict**: Decide which changes to keep. You can:
   - Keep one version of the changes.
   - Combine both changes, if possible, by editing the file manually.

4. **Remove the Conflict Markers**: After resolving the conflict, remove the conflict markers (<<<<<<<, =======, >>>>>>>).

5. **Mark the Conflict as Resolved**: Once you've resolved the conflicts, stage the resolved file(s) using:

bash

git add <file>

6. **Complete the Merge**: After staging the resolved files, commit the changes to complete the merge:

bash

git commit

b. Automating Conflict Resolution with Git Merge Drivers

For simple conflicts (e.g., choosing between one version or the other), you can configure Git to automatically use specific merge strategies via .gitattributes. For example:

- **merge=ours**: Keep changes from the current branch and discard changes from the other branch.
- **merge=theirs**: Keep changes from the other branch and discard changes from the current branch.

Example configuration in .gitattributes:

bash

*.txt merge=ours

This forces Git to always prefer the current branch's changes for .txt files during merges.

4. Tips for Preventing Merge Conflicts in Teams

Preventing merge conflicts is often more efficient than resolving them. Here are several tips to minimize the likelihood of conflicts in a team environment:

a. Communicate Frequently with Your Team

Clear communication is key. Make sure that team members know which parts of the codebase they are working on, and avoid multiple people working on the same file or feature at the same time. Use tools like Slack or team meetings to ensure alignment.

b. Use Feature Branches

Encourage team members to create dedicated feature branches for their work. This minimizes the chance of directly modifying the same code as others. Feature branches can later be merged into the main or develop branch.

c. Pull and Merge Frequently

Regularly pull changes from the main repository to stay up-to-date. By merging frequently, you reduce the chance of long-running branches that might diverge significantly from the main branch, making conflict resolution easier.

d. Avoid Large, Complex Merges

Encourage small, incremental commits that focus on one task or feature at a time. Avoid working on multiple features in a single branch, as this increases the likelihood of conflicts.

e. Use Git Hooks for Pre-Merge Checks

Use pre-commit or pre-push Git hooks to automatically run linting, tests, or checks before commits and pushes. This ensures that code is always in a consistent, error-free state, reducing the chance of conflicts arising from invalid code.

f. Use a Code Review Process

Implement a robust code review process. Reviewing changes before they're merged into the main branch helps identify potential conflicts early and ensures that changes are well-understood and coordinated.

Merge conflicts are an inevitable part of collaborative software development, but by understanding their causes and using the right tools and strategies, they can be resolved efficiently. Regular communication, frequent merging, and the use of feature branches are key practices for preventing conflicts. Additionally, taking advantage of merge tools and Git's conflict resolution mechanisms will help streamline the process when conflicts do occur. By following these best practices, teams can work more effectively, reduce bottlenecks, and maintain a clean, functioning codebase.

CHAPTER 23: OPTIMIZING YOUR GITHUB PROFILE AND REPOSITORIES

GitHub is not just a place to host your code; it's a platform for collaboration, discovery, and community-building, especially when it comes to open-source contributions. Whether you're a developer looking to showcase your personal projects, contribute to others, or build a strong open-source presence, optimizing your GitHub profile and repositories is crucial. This chapter will explore how to build a strong GitHub profile, make your repositories discoverable, and contribute effectively to the open-source community.

1. Building a Strong GitHub Profile for Open-Source Contributions

Your GitHub profile is the digital representation of your work and identity as a developer. It's often the first thing people see when they consider collaborating with you or reviewing your contributions. A strong, professional profile increases your chances of getting noticed by potential collaborators or employers, especially if you're active in open-source.

a. Complete Your Profile Information

A well-completed GitHub profile includes more than just your name and photo. You should provide the following:

- **Profile Picture**: A clear and professional photo makes you more approachable. Alternatively, use a unique logo or avatar that reflects your personality or brand.
- **Bio**: Write a concise and engaging bio. Mention your expertise, interests, and current projects. You can also include links to your personal website or blog, social media profiles, or other relevant platforms (like LinkedIn).
- **Location and Contact Information**: This can help others get in touch with you for collaboration opportunities or job offers. You can also link to your email if you're comfortable with it.
- **Pinned Repositories**: GitHub allows you to pin repositories to your profile, showcasing your best or most significant projects. This is an opportunity to highlight your work that you want others to see first.

b. Highlight Your Contributions

GitHub tracks your contributions across repositories, including issues, pull requests, and commits. Ensure you're making meaningful contributions to both your own and others' projects. Having a consistent history of contributions will help establish credibility and demonstrate your ongoing involvement in the open-source community.

- **Contributions Graph**: The green squares on your GitHub profile represent contributions you've made. Regular activity helps show you're an active participant. Even if you're not coding daily, contribute through comments, reviews, and documentation.

c. Public Repositories vs. Private Repositories

While private repositories are suitable for personal projects, open-source contributions and projects should be in public repositories. Make sure to have at least a few well-documented public repositories that show off your skills and interests. If you're contributing to open-source, most contributions happen in public repositories, and this openness increases your visibility.

2. Making Your Repositories More Discoverable

To increase the visibility of your repositories and attract potential collaborators, it's important to optimize the way your repositories are presented. Here's how to make your projects more discoverable:

a. Use Descriptive and Relevant Repository Names

Your repository name should clearly describe the project's purpose or function. Keep it concise but descriptive. Avoid using vague names like "my-project" or "test-repo." Instead, use names like "personal-finance-tracker" or "python-data-cleaning-tools," which give potential users or contributors a quick understanding of what the project is about.

b. Tag Repositories with Relevant Topics

GitHub allows you to add topics (tags) to your repositories. Topics are keywords that categorize your project, making it easier for others to discover it when they search for relevant terms. You can add tags like "machine-learning," "web-scraping," "flask," "python," etc., depending on the nature of your project.

c. Include a Good Description

Each repository should include a short and clear description that summarizes what the project does and why it's useful. This is the first thing people see when they visit your repo, so it's essential to grab attention with a clear, compelling summary.

d. Maintain a Clean and Organized Repository

Ensure your repository is well-organized and easy to navigate. This includes:

- **Directory structure**: A logical folder structure that separates the core code, documentation, tests, etc.
- **License**: Clearly state the licensing terms for your project. Open-source projects typically use licenses like MIT, Apache, or GPL.
- **Issues**: Keep track of bugs, features, and tasks by using GitHub issues. Clearly categorize them (bug, enhancement, question) and tag them with labels to make the project easier to manage.

e. Ensure Repository is Well-Documented

Good documentation is one of the most important factors in making your repository discoverable and usable. A well-documented project can attract both users and contributors, making it more likely to gain traction.

3. Best Practices for README and Documentation

A great README file is one of the most important aspects of a repository. It sets the tone for how people will engage with your project and is often the first thing people look at when they land on your repository.

a. Clear Project Introduction

The first section of your README should briefly explain what the project is, what it does, and why it's important. This should be a high-level summary that answers these questions:

- What problem does the project solve?
- Who will benefit from using this project?
- What technologies or tools does it use?

b. Installation and Setup Instructions

Ensure that users can easily set up your project. Include clear instructions on how to install and configure the project. This could include installation steps using package managers (e.g., pip, npm, brew) and prerequisites (e.g., specific versions of Python, Node.js, etc.).

Example:

bash

Clone the repository
git clone https://github.com/your-username/project-name.git

Install dependencies
cd project-name
pip install -r requirements.txt

c. Usage Instructions

Provide clear instructions on how to use the project. If the project has a command-line interface (CLI), include example commands. If it's a web application, show how to access it and give sample input/output.

d. Contributing Guidelines

Encourage others to contribute to your project by including a **CONTRIBUTING.md** file. In this section, outline the process for contributing, including:

- Forking the repository and creating a new branch.
- Running tests before submitting pull requests.
- Writing clear commit messages.
- Creating issues for bugs or new features.

e. Licensing

State the license under which the project is distributed. This informs users how they can legally use, modify, and distribute the code. Popular open-source licenses include MIT, Apache 2.0, and GPL-3.0.

f. Badges and Shields

Badges can visually indicate the health of the project, such as build status, test coverage, or license type. Tools like shields.io allow you to add these badges to your README for greater visibility and professionalism.

4. Open-Source Etiquette and Contributing to Other Projects

Contributing to open-source projects is not just about writing code; it's about being part of a community. Open-source etiquette is essential to building a respectful, productive environment.

a. Read the Documentation First

Before contributing to a project, thoroughly read its documentation, including the README and CONTRIBUTING guidelines. Make sure you understand the project's goals, setup instructions, and how to contribute.

b. Start with Issues

If you're unsure where to start, look for open issues that need attention. Many repositories have labels like "good first issue" to help new contributors get started. If there are no issues, consider adding your own (such as a bug or feature request).

c. Fork and Clone

Always fork the repository before making changes, and ensure that your local version is up to date with the latest changes from the main repository. Use git pull to keep your fork synced with the upstream project.

d. Submit Clean Pull Requests

When you submit a pull request (PR), ensure it meets the following standards:

- Make sure the code is well-written and adheres to the project's style guides.
- Write clear and concise commit messages.
- Provide a clear explanation of what your PR does in the description.
- If it's a large change, break it into smaller, more manageable PRs.

e. Respect the Project's Workflow

Different projects have different workflows for reviewing and merging contributions. Some may require pull request reviews, while others may be more permissive. Be sure to follow the project's guidelines for submitting contributions and be patient during the review process.

f. Be Respectful and Open to Feedback

Remember that open-source is a collaborative effort. Be open to feedback on your contributions, and be respectful when discussing issues or suggesting changes. Code reviews are opportunities to improve your skills and learn from others.

Optimizing your GitHub profile and repositories is an essential part of building your open-source presence. By creating an appealing and professional profile, making your repositories discoverable, and contributing to other projects in a respectful and effective manner, you'll attract collaborators and increase the impact of your work. Whether you're sharing personal projects or contributing to large open-source initiatives, following best practices for documentation, etiquette, and visibility will help ensure that your GitHub presence stands out in the developer community.

CHAPTER 24: SUMMARY AND BEST PRACTICES FOR GIT AND GITHUB

Git and GitHub are essential tools for modern software development, offering powerful capabilities for version control, collaboration, and continuous integration. As you progress from basic to advanced topics in Git, it becomes clear that mastery of these tools is crucial for developers working on both individual projects and collaborative team efforts. In this final chapter, we'll summarize key takeaways for mastering Git and GitHub, recap best practices, and provide tips for building an effective Git workflow for both personal and team-based projects. We'll also touch on future trends in version control.

1. Key Takeaways for Mastering Git and GitHub

Mastering Git and GitHub involves understanding the core concepts and tools while also leveraging advanced features for efficient collaboration and development workflows. Here are the key takeaways from the previous chapters:

a. Understanding Git's Core Principles

- **Version Control**: Git enables version tracking, allowing you to manage changes to your codebase and revert to previous versions if necessary. It gives developers a reliable history of changes, which is essential for debugging, collaboration, and feature development.

- **Branches and Merging**: Branching allows you to work on features or fixes in isolation, without affecting the main codebase. Git's merging and rebasing features allow you to integrate these isolated changes back into the main branch efficiently.

- **Commit History**: Commits are snapshots of your project, providing a clear and traceable history of changes. Frequent, meaningful commits ensure that changes are well-documented and easy to roll back if needed.

b. GitHub as a Collaboration Platform

- **Repository Hosting**: GitHub is not just a place to store your code—it's a platform for collaboration. It integrates with Git, providing remote repositories that you can push and pull changes from, facilitating collaboration with other developers.

- **Issues and Pull Requests**: GitHub's issue tracking system allows you to manage bugs, enhancements, and tasks. Pull requests (PRs) enable code review and collaborative merging of changes, making it easy to discuss and refine contributions before they become part of the main codebase.

- **GitHub Actions**: GitHub Actions provides CI/CD functionality directly in GitHub, automating tests, deployments, and other processes to improve your workflow and ensure code quality.

c. Advanced Features for Workflow Efficiency

- **Git Tags and Releases**: Tags mark specific points in your project history, typically used to signal releases. Annotated tags include more information, such as the tagger's name, date, and message, making them a great way to document important project milestones.
- **Git Stash and Reset**: Git stash allows you to save uncommitted changes temporarily, which is particularly useful when switching branches or working on multiple features simultaneously. Git reset and git revert offer powerful ways to undo or modify past commits.
- **Submodules**: Git submodules allow you to include external repositories as part of your project. They are useful for managing dependencies or large projects with multiple repositories.

2. Recap of Best Practices for Version Control

Implementing best practices in Git and GitHub not only makes development smoother but also ensures better collaboration, maintainability, and scalability for your projects.

a. Commit Often and with Clarity

- **Small, Frequent Commits**: Make small, incremental commits regularly. This improves traceability and allows for easier bug isolation. Avoid committing large chunks of code that make it hard to understand what has changed.

- **Descriptive Commit Messages**: Commit messages should be clear and descriptive, summarizing the "what" and "why" of a change. A good commit message should help anyone reading it (including your future self) understand the purpose of the change.

b. Branching and Merging

- **Use Feature Branches**: Always create feature branches for new work, whether it's a new feature, bug fix, or experimental change. This keeps the main branch clean and production-ready.

- **Merge Often**: Regularly merge changes from the main branch into your feature branches to stay up to date and avoid large, difficult merges at the end of development.

- **Resolve Conflicts Early**: When merging, resolve conflicts as soon as possible. Git's three-way merge or tools like git mergetool can help, but frequent merging minimizes the likelihood of complex conflicts.

c. Collaboration via Pull Requests

- **Use Pull Requests for Collaboration**: When working in teams, always submit pull requests for changes. This enables team members to review code, suggest improvements, and ensure consistency before changes are merged.

- **Be Clear in Your PR Descriptions**: Include a description of the changes you've made and any context necessary for reviewers to understand why the changes are needed. Link to relevant issues, and be open to feedback.

- **Review PRs Thoughtfully**: Review others' pull requests carefully, paying attention to the code quality, design decisions, and possible bugs. Leave constructive comments to improve the code.

d. Keep Repositories Clean and Organized

- **Use .gitignore Files**: Always include a .gitignore file in your project to exclude unnecessary files (e.g., build files, configuration files, or IDE settings) from version control. This keeps your repository clean and focused on the source code.

- **Document Everything**: Provide clear, concise documentation in your README file. Include setup instructions, usage examples, and contribute guidelines. Well-documented projects are easier for others to understand and contribute to.

e. Security and Authentication

- **Use SSH Keys for Authentication**: SSH keys provide secure authentication to GitHub, eliminating the need for repeated password entry.
- **Enable Two-Factor Authentication (2FA)**: Add an extra layer of security to your GitHub account by enabling 2FA.
- **Be Mindful of Sensitive Data**: Never commit sensitive information like passwords, API keys, or secrets to version control. Use environment variables or secret management tools instead.

3. Building a Git Workflow for Individual and Team Projects

a. Individual Git Workflow

As an individual developer, your Git workflow is focused on managing your own changes and maintaining a clean, consistent history:

- **Create a new branch for each feature or task**.
- **Commit frequently and push often** to ensure your work is backed up and you can access it from multiple machines.
- **Merge or rebase regularly** to ensure your branches stay up to date with the latest changes from the main branch.
- **Use tags for important milestones**, such as version releases.

b. Team Git Workflow

In a team setting, collaboration becomes the focus. A common team-based Git workflow is **Git Flow**, which works well for teams that work on multiple features and release cycles:

- **Master Branch**: This is the production-ready code that contains the stable version of the project.
- **Develop Branch**: This branch contains the latest development code, and all feature branches get merged into it.
- **Feature Branches**: Each new feature should be developed in its own branch, which is merged into develop once complete.
- **Release Branches**: Used to prepare for production releases, allowing bug fixes and small changes without affecting the develop branch.
- **Hotfix Branches**: These are used to quickly fix bugs on the master branch, typically in response to urgent issues.

Tools like **GitHub Actions** or **CircleCI** can automate aspects of this workflow, such as testing and deployment, making it easier to manage continuous integration and deployment.

4. Future Trends and Tools for Version Control in Development

Version control tools, including Git and GitHub, are evolving rapidly. While Git remains the most popular system, other tools and trends are shaping the future of development workflows:

a. Improved Collaboration Tools

GitHub is continuously adding new features to improve collaboration, such as GitHub Actions for CI/CD, code scanning, and advanced issue tracking. GitHub is also adding more integrations with external tools, enabling a smoother development lifecycle.

b. AI and Automation in Version Control

Artificial intelligence and machine learning will increasingly be integrated into version control tools. For example, AI could be used to automatically suggest code improvements or detect security vulnerabilities in code before it's merged.

c. Distributed Version Control with Enhanced Security

As security concerns continue to grow, we can expect more tools focused on enhancing the security of version control systems. This includes better support for managing secrets, improved audit trails, and tools for ensuring code integrity in decentralized environments.

d. Integration with Cloud and DevOps Pipelines

Version control systems will continue to integrate seamlessly with cloud platforms and DevOps pipelines. GitHub, GitLab, and others are already providing integrated CI/CD pipelines that automate testing and deployment, making it easier to build and ship software faster.

Mastering Git and GitHub is a fundamental skill for modern developers, whether working alone or as part of a team. By following best practices—such as frequent, clear commits, using branching strategies, collaborating through pull requests, and securing your repositories—you'll be able to build a robust version control system that enhances your productivity and collaboration. Looking forward, the future of version control will continue to be shaped by cloud integration, AI-powered features, and improved security. Embrace these trends to stay ahead of the curve and make your Git and GitHub workflow even more efficient and secure.

www.ingramcontent.com/pod-product-compliance
Lightning Source LLC
LaVergne TN
LVHW052128070326
832902LV00039B/4128